ARIANA

Grande

HEARST
HOME

Ariana performs a medley of "Imagine," "My Favorite Things," "7 Rings," and "Thank U, Next" at the 62nd Annual Grammy Awards.

ARIANA
Grande

THE RISE
OF A
DANGEROUS
WOMAN

By Maura Johnston,
with essays by Joel Calfee,
Katie Connor, and
Lisa Whittington-Hill

HEARST
HOME

Contents

RIGHT Ariana attends the EE BAFTA Film Awards at the Royal Festival Hall on February 16, 2025, in London. She was nominated for Best Supporting Actress for her role as Glinda in *Wicked*.

Ariana attends the European premiere of *Wicked* at the Royal Festival Hall in London on November 18, 2024. For this final premiere event, Ariana opted for a butter-yellow Ralph Lauren gown—a break from the "Glinda pink" she wore during previous appearances.

Chapter
1

WHY ARIANA, WHY NOW?

She Contains Multitudes

Child star. Pop diva. Feminist activist. Cosmetics and perfume magnate. Devoted daughter, sister, and granddaughter. Four-octave phenomenon. Vocal impressionist. Comedic genius. Grammy Award winner. Oscar-nominated movie star. Just a nice Italian girl from Boca. But who is the real Ari?

WILL THE REAL ARIANA PLEASE STAND UP

The easiest answer is that the real Ariana Grande is a singer. While she first became a celebrity thanks to her role as Cat Valentine on Nickelodeon's *Victorious* and its spin-off *Sam & Cat*, what Ariana really yearned to do was sing. "I don't remember a time in my life when I wasn't singing," she said on NPR's *Fresh Air* in 2025. "As soon as I could speak, I was singing."

In 2010 Ariana got her chance. She sang with her close friend and *Victorious* castmate Elizabeth Gillies on a *Victorious* compilation, and in 2011 she released her first solo single, "Put Your Hearts Up." Both were bubblegum pop, which didn't align with Ariana's vision. She wanted to record an album with more of an R&B sound, like her musical heroes Mariah Carey and Whitney Houston. Ariana wanted to be taken seriously as a singer, to become more than a child star.

MUSIC COMES FIRST

While still filming *Victorious*, Ariana started uploading her covers of Adele, Whitney, and Mariah songs to YouTube. These caught the attention of a label exec at Republic Records, who signed her, and she released her first album, *Yours Truly*, in 2013. From the beginning of her career, her focus was on the music: "If I could, I would not do anything else," she told *Elle* weeks before the album came out. "I'd just be in the studio for my whole life. I would never go to parties, events, and red carpets. I would rather just be in the studio for the whole time. I don't even care. Nobody has to know what I look like. I just want to make music." *Yours Truly* debuted at the top spot on the *Billboard* 200 and would be the first of many number ones for Ariana, whose rare four-octave vocal range hits higher than her signature ponytail.

More than a decade since that first album, Ariana's musical success includes seven studio albums, two Grammy Awards, twelve Teen Choice Awards, ten MTV Video Music Awards, and sales of more than 90 million albums worldwide. That girl with dreams of being a singer has emerged as more than just a pop star—she's a vocal super-talent who doesn't give up on her dreams.

RIGHT Ariana hits the stage in Toronto during her first world tour in 2015. The Honeymoon Tour supported her first two studio albums, *Yours Truly* and *My Everything*. It kicked off in Missouri and finished in Brazil. "Good music, good choreography, and a great time—I want to make sure that my fans have the best night of their lives," Ariana told audiences in a video that opened each night's performance.

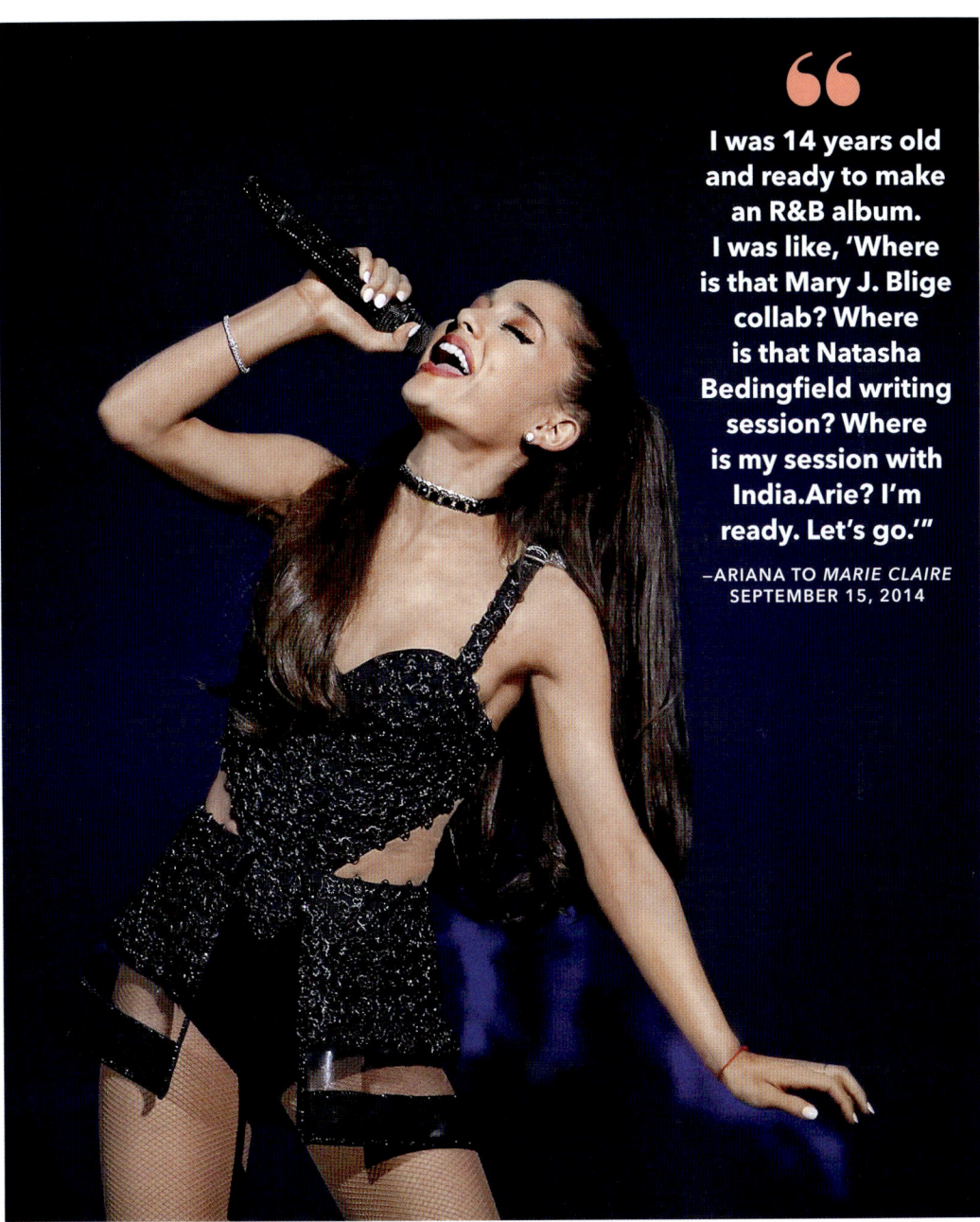

> **I was 14 years old and ready to make an R&B album. I was like, 'Where is that Mary J. Blige collab? Where is that Natasha Bedingfield writing session? Where is my session with India.Arie? I'm ready. Let's go.'"**
>
> —ARIANA TO *MARIE CLAIRE*
> SEPTEMBER 15, 2014

A DRAMA KID FROM THE START

The real Ariana is also an actress. Her biggest role yet has been playing Glinda in the 2024 release of the musical *Wicked*, but Ariana's journey to the yellow brick road started when she was eight. She performed in Boca Raton community theater, starring as Annie in the Little Palm Family Theatre's production of the musical of the same name and as Dorothy in *The Wizard of Oz* at the Crest Theatre in Delray Beach. She made her Broadway debut in *13*, which won her a National Youth Theatre Association Award, but Ariana has always had Glinda on the brain. Growing up in Florida, she sang the lyrics to *Wicked* while riding in the back of her parents' car, and in a post-performance backstage meeting with Kristin Chenoweth, *Wicked*'s original Glinda on Broadway from 2003 to 2004, ten-year-old Ariana told her she wanted to play the role someday. When the movie adaptation was announced in 2012, Ariana, then nineteen, was determined to land the part and immersed herself in all things Good Witch. On the *Zach Sang Show* in 2024, she confessed to "hunting" producer Marc Platt. "I was like, 'Hey, I don't know when this is happening, but when it's happening, may I please at least just audition?' That's all I wanted, was an audition. I've never wanted anything more."

In an industry seemingly ruled by ego and entitlement, and contrary to the public criticism of divaism sometimes directed toward her, Ariana's dedication might come as a surprise. But despite all her achievements, Ariana doesn't take success for granted. She fights for what she wants, every step of the way.

Once auditions for the movie finally got going in 2021, Ariana proved just how badly she wanted the role by undertaking an intense, six-month preparation process for her audition. Zach Sang said it was like she was "training for the Super Bowl."

That training included daily acting lessons and work with a vocal coach to deconstruct her singing voice so she could adopt the operatic style required for the movie. Her preparations also involved winning over the at-first-skeptical director Jon M. Chu, who initially questioned whether Ariana had the acting chops needed for a big film. Despite playing small parts in *Don't Look Up* and *Zoolander 2* and a host of appearances on *Saturday Night Live*, *The Tonight Show Starring Jimmy Fallon*, and other venues that proved her astounding talent for vocal impressions and comedic chops, *Wicked* would be Ariana's first leading movie role. After multiple auditions—for at least one she prepared and sang songs and ran lines for both the Elphaba part and Glinda (although she never seriously considered the role of Elphaba, saying "I secretly knew that I was only meant for Glinda")—she won the part. It was proof she was more than just a pint-sized pop star with a powerhouse voice. Ariana is a hardworking actress who prepares—hard—for her roles.

THE REAL REAL ARIANA

But Ariana is also . . . *real*. Fans love her openness on social media, where Ariana's posts feel honest and authentic. One *New York Times* piece called her "a master of the Easter egg, the clapback, the strategic tweet-and-delete." She is one of the most followed female celebrities on Instagram and YouTube and has used her platforms to raise awareness about social issues and causes. She has advocated for LGBTQIA+ rights and spoken out against discrimination and intolerance. Ariana has a close relationship with her family and has credited her openly gay brother, Frankie Grande, with inspiring her LGBTQIA+ activism. She speaks candidly in the press and on social media about her struggles with obsessive compulsive disorder, depression, and anxiety, even though celebrities are sometimes mocked for doing so.

"I think it's important to speak up about issues that matter, and I believe we all have a responsibility to use our voices to help make a difference," Ariana told *Miss Vogue* back in 2016. "I wish people would be nicer to one another, especially on social media where comments can be so cruel."

Ariana has also called attention to the double standard that female celebrities experience. In 2015 she posted a feminist manifesto on Twitter that slammed the media's gender bias, saying, "If a woman has a lot of sex (or any sex for that matter) . . . she's a 'slut.' If a man has sex . . . HE'S. A. STUD. A BOSSSSSS. a KING. If a woman even TALKS about sex openly . . . she is shamed!" She's criticized the paparazzi and the tabloid press for their relentless coverage of her romantic relationships over her accomplishments and urged the media to focus more on a woman's art than her appearance. In a 2023 TikTok post, Ariana implored people to "be gentler and less comfortable commenting on people's bodies, no matter what." During the press tour for *Wicked*, Ariana discussed the emotional toll the constant focus on her appearance has taken on her. "I've been a specimen in a petri dish really since I was sixteen or seventeen. I have heard it all. I've heard every version of it—of what's wrong with me. And then you fix it, and it's wrong for different reasons."

Ariana continues to be one of the most outspoken and introspective celebrities—a fierce and loyal advocate for other women in the business.

THE FULL PACKAGE

So the real Ariana is so much more complex than her job descriptions. She's talented, determined, dedicated, outspoken, introspective, and authentic. Throughout her career, Ariana has shown us that she does in fact contain multitudes. And in the process, she's become a legend. 🦋

By Lisa Whittington-Hill

RIGHT Ariana attends and is a surprise performer at the 76th annual Met Gala, held on May 6, 2024. She was a dream straight out of the "Sleeping Beauties: Reawakening Fashion" theme. As she was carried to the stage—her head on a pillow, à la *Sleeping Beauty*— by an entourage of fairies, she performed "Once Upon a Dream" from the original Disney classic.

Ariana's Rise

Twelve moments define her trajectory to the very top.

BY MAURA JOHNSTON

1

JUNE 26, 1993
Ariana Grande-Butera is born in Boca Raton, Florida, to marine communications CEO Joan Grande (left, with Ariana) and graphic designer Edward Butera. To this day, Ari identifies deeply with the idyllic coastal community, referring to herself as "just a girl from Boca who loves art" in a 2025 *Hollywood Reporter* interview.

JANUARY 21, 2007
Ariana starts the YouTube account ohsnapitzari–"oh snap, it's Ari"–where she posts vlogs, responses to YouTube-wide challenges, movie parodies, and, eventually, covers of tracks like Mariah Carey's "Emotions" and Rihanna's "Only Girl (In the World)." (The account eventually transitioned to her official YouTube, where it has more than 55 million subscribers. She ranks among the top solo artists on the platform, including Justin Bieber, pictured here with Ari at Coachella in 2019.)

2

3

OCTOBER 5, 2008
After runs in Los Angeles and Connecticut and a string of preview performances, *13* opens at the Bernard B. Jacobs Theatre on Broadway. Ariana plays the popular cheerleader Charlotte in the musical, which makes history as the first Broadway production to have its entire cast and band made up of teenagers.

I remember a day [in rehearsal] with everyone going around the piano and just improvising, and some of them clearly were like, I have no idea how to improvise a solo. And some of them were Ariana Grande."

—*13* COMPOSER JASON ROBERT BROWN
TO *THE NEW YORK TIMES*, AUGUST 15, 2022

4

[T]he best *Victorious* moments tended to focus on a Cat side-adventure with another contrasting supporting character."

—ANDREW UNTERBERGER ON ARIANA'S PORTRAYAL OF CAT VALENTINE IN *VICTORIOUS*, *BILLBOARD*, AUGUST 22, 2014

MARCH 27, 2010
The teen sitcom *Victorious*, starring Victoria Justice as aspiring performer Tori Vega, airs on Nickelodeon. Ariana—making her debut as a TV regular—plays the bubbly, flame-haired Cat Valentine. She reprises the role in the spin-off *Sam & Cat*, which makes Ariana a household name for tween girls.

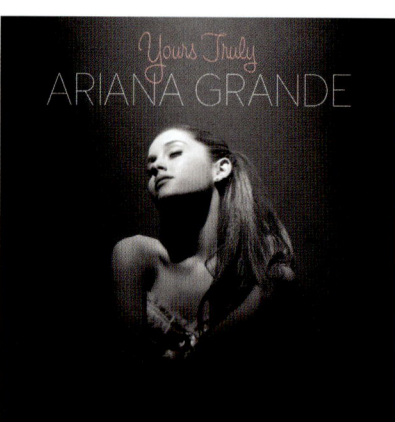

5

AUGUST 30, 2013
Ariana releases her debut solo album, *Yours Truly*. Inspired by the R&B and hip-hop that she grew up on and that influenced her singing style, it's a commercial and critical hit. It leads to Ariana's first top-ten single, the Mac Miller (below)-assisted confection "The Way," and establishes her as an up-and-coming force in pop.

6

FEBRUARY 25, 2015
The Honeymoon
Tour, Ariana's first
headlining world
tour, kicks off at
the Independence
Events Center in
Independence,
Missouri. The show's
set list puts the
spotlight on hits
from *Yours Truly*
and its follow-up,
My Everything, with
some nights featuring
cover songs and
drop-ins from guests
like Big Sean and
Justin Bieber.

SEPTEMBER 16, 2015

Ariana launches her first fragrance, the "beautiful, feminine, and flirty all at the same time" Ari by Ariana Grande. In the years that follow, Ariana amasses more than $1 billion in scent sales thanks to her steadily releasing perfumes like Sweet Like Candy and Mod Vanilla. In 2021, she launches r.e.m. beauty, a line of skincare and cosmetics that quickly becomes a critical and commercial favorite.

8

JUNE 4, 2017

The Ariana-organized One Love Manchester, a benefit concert responding to the terrorist bombing of Ariana's May 22 concert in the English city of Manchester, raises more than £17 million (almost $23 million) for charities supporting victims of the bombing and their families. The lineup includes Miley Cyrus, Stevie Wonder, Mac Miller, Coldplay, and Justin Bieber.

9

NOVEMBER 17, 2018

Ariana's gossamer relationship retrospective "Thank U, Next" from her album *Sweetener* debuts at No. 1 on the *Billboard* Hot 100 chart, giving Ariana her first No. 1 single and first chart-topping debut. Its follow-up single, the "My Favorite Things"–quoting "7 Rings," debuts at the singles chart's summit two months later.

10

APRIL 14, 2019
Ariana headlines
Coachella, one of
the world's leading
music and arts
festivals (and invites
guests and friends
like Nicki Minaj, left,
to perform). Ariana
is the fourth solo
woman to headline
the festival and,
at the time, the
youngest headliner.

11

NOVEMBER 2021
Ariana, pictured here with director Jon M. Chu (left) and costar
Cynthia Erivo (right), announces that she's been cast as Galinda
Upland, a.k.a. Glinda the Good Witch, for the film version of
Wicked. For the next three years Ariana immerses herself in Oz
while still making time to record a new studio album, *Eternal
Sunshine*, which releases in 2024.

She has such a clear vision about what she wants to do and how to do it."

—CYNTHIA ERIVO TO *VANITY FAIR*, SEPTEMBER 30, 2024

12

NOVEMBER 22, 2024
Wicked opens in theaters around the world. Playing opposite British actor and singer Cynthia Erivo, Ariana receives critical accolades and, eventually, an Academy Award nomination for Best Supporting Actress. She doesn't win, but she does open the 2025 Oscars telecast alongside Erivo, with the two duetting on an Oz-themed medley.

Ariana takes the mic during curtain call at the opening performance of the Broadway musical *13* on October 5, 2008. A member of the ensemble cast, Ariana was recognized early for her singing talent. "She was as gifted a singer at fourteen as she is now," said the musical's composer, Jason Robert Brown.

Chapter 2

THE THEATER KID

Natural Star Power

Some audiences may have been surprised to suddenly see pop diva Ariana Grande emerge in 2024 as a serious actress, but true fans have been there from the start. From the beginning, Ariana showed every sign of being a gifted actor: as the lead in a local theater production of *Annie*, as a member of the ensemble cast of *13* on Broadway, and eventually as Cat Valentine in Nickelodeon's *Victorious* and *Sam & Cat*. *Harper's Bazaar* writer Joel Calfee, a self-proclaimed Ariana stan, reflects on why Ariana's Oscar nomination for *Wicked* put her comedic and dramatic talents in the spotlight.

Ariana Grande is officially an Oscar-nominated actress, and for months before her nomination, I told anyone who would listen that this would happen.

It's hard being a stan. You spend your days going back and forth with KatyCats and Barbz on social media, you lose hundreds on vinyl variants, and suffer from constant dry mouth because you can't help but sing along every time you step into a department store and hear "No Tears Left to Cry" on the loudspeakers.

Most people aren't cut out for this work, but I am. The only problem is that I never know when it might cloud my judgment. To be honest, I knew I would love Grande's performance as Glinda long before I stepped into the theater to see the film adaptation of *Wicked*. She could have done vocal runs in front of a white wall for 160 minutes and I still

would have cheered and called her "Mother" on my Letterboxd.

But the minute Grande floated onto the screen in that giant pink bubble, I realized it wasn't just pop fanaticism. The truth is that Grande is a triumph. She takes a character that's totally one-note in *The Wizard of Oz* and gives her supreme depth. Her deliveries are hilarious, her moments of sincerity ring true, and she can't help but steal every scene she's in. It's hard to fill the shoes of a monolith like Kristin Chenoweth, but Grande comfortably holds her own.

Clearly, I wasn't the only one impressed by the pop star's acting, because when *Wicked* came out, the reviews quickly glowed as bright as her bubble. And perhaps the greatest recognition arrived on January 23, 2025, when the Academy of Motion Picture Arts and Sciences announced

LEFT In October 2009, Ariana arrives at the premiere of 20th Century Fox's film *Fantastic Mr. Fox*. One of her first red-carpet appearances, a young Ariana had just begun filming for the Nickelodeon ensemble series *Victorious*.

that Grande was nominated in the category for Best Supporting Actress.

"I cannot stop crying, to no one's surprise," she gushed on social media immediately following the news. "I'm humbled and deeply honored to be in such brilliant company and sharing this with tiny Ari who sat and studied Judy Garland singing 'Somewhere Over the Rainbow' just before the big, beautiful bubble entered. I'm so proud of you, tiny."

With her role in *Wicked*, Grande—who has been a theater kid practically since she was in diapers—finally got to show off her true comedic chops. From rolling around on the floor while giving Elphaba (Cynthia Erivo) a makeover, to adding a subtle trill to her words during plain conversations, it's clear that her intuitions as an actor are smart. Though, those who have been paying close attention could've told you that Grande was a true comedienne long ago.

Over a month before *Wicked* hit theaters, the "Yes, And?" singer hosted the October 12, 2024, episode of *Saturday Night Live*, where she did everything from

playing a competitive mother who takes a game of charades too far to delivering a spot-on impression of Jennifer Coolidge. The skits were kooky and outrageous, and Grande totally committed to every second—it was one of the funniest episodes I'd seen in years.

But her comedy started long before that. In recent years, there's been no shortage of playfulness in Grande's music. She never shies away from a cheeky joke—be it naming a song "34+35" (add those numbers together), or claiming that one night with her will make a lover "believe God is a woman." And let's not forget her "Thank U, Next" music video, which paid homage to early aughts rom-coms with silly jokes and star cameos, effectively breaking the internet in the process.

Of course, the biggest hesitations around Grande's acting talents stemmed from the fact that before *Wicked*, her main role was that of the foolish and fiery-haired Cat Valentine on the Nickelodeon series *Victorious*, and later, its spin-off, *Sam & Cat*. Granted, I don't think it's

I remember, even at a very young age, loving the feeling of making people laugh. It was a different kind of connection."

–ARIANA TO *SCREEN INTERNATIONAL*, FEBRUARY 2025

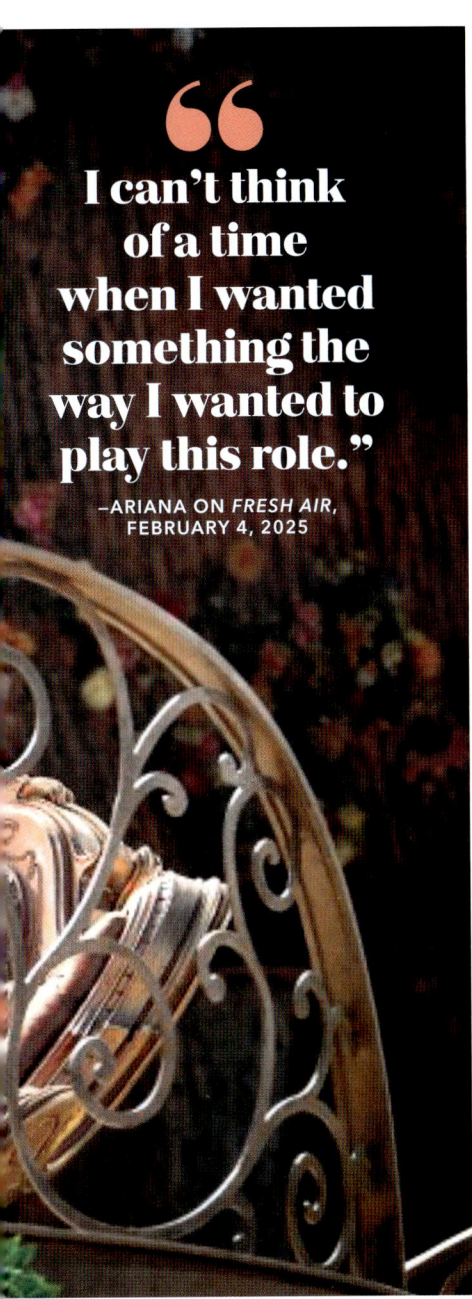

> ## "I can't think of a time when I wanted something the way I wanted to play this role."
>
> —ARIANA ON *FRESH AIR*, FEBRUARY 4, 2025

LEFT Ariana sparkles as Glinda. She describes playing the role in *Wicked* as a return to her theater-kid roots. Ariana began performing at an early age, starting with musical theater in Boca Raton before hitting Broadway.

fair to judge an actor for work they did as a teenager on a show geared toward kids, but when I revisited *Victorious* recently (my nieces have become obsessed), I saw glimpses of the superstar's comedic prowess even then. Want proof? Watch any number of scenes from *Victorious*, which perfectly show off Grande's physical comedy.

The truth is, the public always likes to judge whenever a pop star tries to make the transition to the big screen (they can't all be Lady Gagas or Jennifer Hudsons). But with Grande, the doubt also stemmed from her pairing with Erivo, a respected force in theater, who was on the fast track to earning an EGOT before filming even began (and who gives a magnetic performance as Elphaba, which earned her her own Oscar nod). Even once it became clear that Grande had the talent to act alongside Erivo, the Academy has historically neglected comedic performances—especially those from women—with rare exceptions like Marisa Tomei in *My Cousin Vinny* or Olivia Colman in *The Favourite*.

But all those doubts aside, with her nomination, the world got to see that Grande's casting in *Wicked* was Oscar-worthy, and that her wit is not to be underestimated. And as a stan, well, I'm just glad to see one of the brightest stars of our generation getting her flowers—and thankful to know it wasn't all in my head. 🦋

By Joel Calfee for Harper's Bazaar, 2024

THE COMEDIAN

ARI HAS APPEARED on *The Tonight Show Starring Jimmy Fallon* fifteen times. Not only has she performed her own hits, she's become known for her ability to flip the styles of other pop smashes in the Musical Genre Challenge and impersonate the likes of Christina Aguilera and Céline Dion after spinning the Wheel of Musical Impressions. She's also shown off her teen-sitcom-honed comedic talent in skits and bits alongside the *Saturday Night Live* alum, co-hosting talk show parodies like the teen chat hour "Ew!" and the braggy "No Big Deal," and "Ariana Grande's Ponytail Has a Mind of Its Own," which reveals her ponytail's crime-fighting prowess (and its surprisingly grizzled voice). She once engaged in a conversation with Fallon entirely through lip-synced pop songs, her musical agility and wit on full display.

Ariana has also shown off her comedic skills in *Saturday Night Live* skits about the Kids' Choice Awards and "feminist" songs, played Jennifer Lawrence in the *SNL* perennial "Celebrity Jeopardy," and did a star turn as an intern for the streaming service Tidal who was charged with "filling in" for Britney Spears, Rihanna, and Whitney Houston after some server malfunctions. Ari's imitations were startlingly convincing—and these appearances, among others, confirmed that Ariana was not only one of the best singers of her generation but witty and funny as well.

FAR LEFT Over the years Ariana has shown up in a number of scene-stealing cameos, including playing Chanel #2 in the 2015 TV series *Scream Queens* (featuring TV's slowest-moving, social-media-choreographed murder scene).

TOP In a sunny video with James Corden on *The Late Late Show with James Corden* she celebrates the end of COVID lockdowns.

BOTTOM Ari charms as Piccola Grande, the Pickle Fairy of Hope, on the tragicomedy *Kidding*, starring Jim Carrey, Judy Greer, and Catherine Keener.

LEFT (TOP AND BOTTOM) The role of Annie was one of Ariana's first star performances. The musical was staged by the Little Palm Family Theatre in Boca Raton, Florida, in 2002. After the theater closed, Ariana's mom, Joan, founded a children's troupe called Kids Who Care. "She was an amazing little talent in person," songwriter and family friend Dennis Lambert recalled of her early performances to *The Palm Beach Report*. "She knows how to deliver."

RIGHT Ariana and her *13* castmates attend a handprint ceremony at Planet Hollywood in Times Square in October 2008. Among the group was her longtime Boca theater friend Aaron Simon Gross. The two performed together in Kids Who Care and were thrilled when they both got parts in *13*. They remain close friends.

ABOVE Ariana poses with her *13* castmates backstage on November 5, 2008. From left to right: Elizabeth Gillies, Mark Indelicato, Ariana, and Miranda Cosgrove.

"Two words: Legen. Dary."

—@JIMMYFALLON ON INSTAGRAM ABOUT ARIANA'S TALENT, NOVEMBER 17, 2024

RIGHT In April 2010, Ariana promotes season 1 of *Victorious* at Planet Hollywood in Times Square. Fans loved Ariana's portrayal of Cat Valentine and the series was renewed for season 2. The premiere for the following season was watched by more than 6 million people and was the show's most watched episode.

TOP LEFT Ariana—hair dyed Cat's signature red-velvet color—greets fans as she attends a CD signing for *Victorious: Music from the Hit TV Show* at a Walmart in Duarte, California, on August 13, 2011. This was Ariana's second soundtrack album—she also sang on the cast album for *13*.

BOTTOM LEFT Ari laughs with cast and crew between takes on the set of *Victorious* in February 2011. Despite ongoing rumors about discord and jealousy among the young actors in the show, many of them remain close to Ariana.

RIGHT Ariana and her family attend the opening night of *Born Yesterday* in April 2011. The musical was produced by her brother, Frankie. Pictured here from left to right, are Ariana's grandfather Frank; her mother, Joan; her brother, Frankie; Ariana; and her grandmother Marjorie.

> ## One of my favorite things about Cat was that she never lost her sense of wonder."

—ARIANA ON FACEBOOK (AFTER THE SHOW
WAS CANCELED), JULY 13, 2014

ABOVE Ariana and her brother, Frankie, pose at Planet Hollywood on December 22, 2011. Ariana credits Frankie with being a strong influence in her life, on everything from her love of musical theater to her outspoken support of LGBTQIA+ rights. Ten years older than Ariana, Frankie was the first Grande sibling to pursue musical theater and is both an actor and a theater producer.

LEFT Ariana shows off her bedroom at one of several Hollywood homes she and her mom (and her brother when he was in town) rented while she filmed *Victorious*. This large Tudor was once the home of Francis Ford Coppola.

LEFT Jennette McCurdy and Ariana promote *Sam & Cat* at Planet Hollywood Times Square on May 14, 2013. The show, which premiered on June 8, picks up as Sam Puckett (McCurdy) rescues Cat (Grande) from the back of a garbage truck. The two become roommates and start an after-school babysitting service, and hijinks ensue.

RIGHT Ariana graces the purple-and-orange carpet wearing an Alice + Olivia by Stacey Bendet dress at the 2013 Nickelodeon Kids' Choice Awards in Los Angeles. She and Jennette McCurdy presented the award for Favorite TV Actress to winner Selena Gomez.

Born on the same day a year apart, co-stars Jennette McCurdy and Ariana Grande celebrate their twenty-first and twentieth birthdays (respectively) on the set of *Sam & Cat* on June 26, 2013. While the actors are all smiles, their off-screen relationship was more complicated. McCurdy recollected in her best-selling memoir that she resented Ariana's success at the time.

Ariana accepts the award for Favorite TV Actress from Chris Rock and his daughter Zahra, at Nickelodeon's Kids' Choice Awards in March 2014. *Sam & Cat* also won Favorite TV Show, but just a few short months later, the show would be canceled. When it ended, Ariana thanked her colleagues and fans in a Facebook post and said of her character, Cat, "She always saw negative obstacles as opportunities to make things good."

> **I love making music, but it's a different type of fulfillment when you're working on telling a story with a hundred other people and you're a part of the big picture."**

—ARIANA TO
COSMOPOLITAN
IN MARCH 2017

Ariana poses in a promotional shot for the John Waters–inspired *Hairspray Live!* She returned to her Broadway musical roots for the show, which aired on NBC on December 7, 2016. Ariana played sidekick Penny Pingleton alongside an all-star cast that included Ariana's *Wicked* inspiration, Kristin Chenoweth. *Variety* called Ariana the show's MVP.

In the satirical comedy *Don't Look Up*, Ariana takes the stage as Riley Bina, an exaggerated version of her own star persona. In the film, Ariana does a hilarious send-up of an over-the-top pop star whose romantic breakup overshadows the impending end of the world as an asteroid is on target to destroy Earth. Ariana was given credit for improvising many of her lines, including some of the lyrics she sings in a climactic concert scene with Kid Cudi.

SETTING HER SIGHTS ON OZ

YEARS BEFORE SHE was cast in *Wicked*, Ariana had a strong connection to Oz. As a child it was one of her favorite musicals, and she has described her life as divided into before and after seeing *Wicked* at age ten. Her professional connection to Oz started when she played Dorothy in the *Wizard of Oz* for a local theater production in Boca Raton in 2003. It continued during a *Victorious* episode that riffed on *The Wizard of Oz* and had Ariana's Cat Valentine in Dorothy mode. In 2012 the British singer Mika recruited her for "Popular Song," a bright track that interpolated the *Wicked* song "Popular," and in 2018 she took on an Elphaba cut from the play when she sang "The Wizard and I" on the fifteenth-anniversary celebration, *A Very Wicked Halloween*. Ariana has performed the Judy Garland standard "Over the Rainbow" multiple times, including closing One Love Manchester with the song.

In a March 2012 *Victorious* April Fool's Day episode, the kids perform "The Wizard of Wazz." Ariana played Dorothy to her co-star Victoria Justice's (Tori Vega) Good Witch.

A single of the song was released, and its proceeds went to a charity established for the victims and families of the bombing. The song was also added to the Dangerous Woman Tour's set list.

When she turned thirty, she posted a picture of herself as a young girl, wearing a blue gingham dress that recalled *Oz* heroine Dorothy.

And Ariana sang "Over the Rainbow" once again at the Oscars as part of a tribute to Oz that also featured her and co-star Cynthia Erivo duetting on "Defying Gravity."

No one in the audience could help but notice her smile as she sang this line: "And the dreams that you dare to dream really do come true."

TOP Ariana channeled her Oz inspiration, Judy Garland, at the 2025 Oscars, wearing a ruby-slipper-inspired dress and singing the song Garland made famous, "Over the Rainbow." Since childhood, she's worked to emulate the singer: "Every day, my mom and I would watch a different Judy Garland VHS. I love how she tells a story when she sings. It was just about her voice and the words she was singing—no strings attached or silly hair or costumes, just a woman singing her heart out."

BOTTOM LEFT Ariana attends the 2011 Los Angeles premiere of *Wicked* at the Pantages Theatre. She caught the show again as recently as 2022, when she herself was already in production for the movie.

BOTTOM RIGHT At the Australian premiere for *Wicked* on November 3, 2024, in Sydney, Ariana wears a butterfly choker similar to the one worn by Billie Burke, the original Glinda, in the 1939 film *The Wizard of Oz*.

RED-CARPET STYLE

Ariana goes for a sophisticated look in a red halter dress at the 2012 Creative Arts Emmy Awards on September 15, at the Nokia Theatre.

Since Ariana first hit the red carpet while portraying Cat Valentine in Nickelodeon's *Victorious*, she has been known for a distinct aesthetic: teetering heels or over-the-knee boots; short dresses, often with a flared skirt; and high ponytail. But as she has matured, so has her look—the ponytail may still be in evidence, but it is colored or curled according to the effect she is creating, and her hemlines and silhouettes now project a sophisticated and iconic star, with occasional nods to her pop-star roots or current projects.

> **Ariana Grande's style has transformed throughout her career, reflecting her growth as an artist and individual."**
>
> —RENAN BOTELHO, *WWD*, JANUARY 4, 2025

This classic Ariana silhouette in a floral pattern was designed by Kenley Collins for the 2013 MTV Video Music Awards on August 25.

At the 2014 MTV Video Music Awards on August 24, Ariana pairs a Moschino dress and Tom Ford boots.

Ariana stuns in a sophisticated white and silver mesh floor-length dress by Versace on the 2015 Grammy Awards red carpet on February 8.

For the 58th Annual Grammys, held on February 15, 2016, Ariana wears a fit-and-flared red dress by Romona Keveza.

Ariana looks heavenly in a custom Vera Wang gown at the Met Gala on May 7, 2018.

Ariana elevates her look in Christian Siriano for the 2018 *Billboard* Women in Music event, where she wins Woman of the Year.

On January 26, 2020, Ariana seems to float in a multitiered tulle Giambattista Valli gown for the 62nd Annual Grammys.

For the 96th Academy Awards on March10, 2024, Ariana again wears Giambattista Valli.

Ariana arrives at the 2024 Met Gala on May 6, in a custom Loewe gown with a mother-of-pearl corseted bodice.

For the Oscars on March 2, 2025, Ariana shines in a Schiaparelli gown from the spring 2025 couture collection. The gauzy skirt beneath the fitted bodice features over 190,000 crystals.

59

Ariana performs during the opening night of the Dangerous Woman Tour in Phoenix on February 3, 2017. "As impressive as her show two years ago was at the time, that was actually nothing compared to this year's model," the *Arizona Republic* wrote in a review. "It was clear that the singer had grown from a former child star in transition . . . into a self-assured R&B diva with the vocal chops to back up the confident swagger she brought to the stage on that opening number."

Chapter
3

THE
HITMAKER

Her Musical Evolution

When Ariana Grande made her first moves toward embarking on a pop career, she had a definite goal in mind: She wanted to make an R&B album in the vein of India.Arie, whose introspective cuts like "Video" made her one of neo-soul's premier singer-songwriters and whose music Ariana had discovered while mainlining music as a child. She told the managers she'd been working with, and they were incredulous at the then-fourteen-year-old's moxie. "They were like, 'Um, that's a helluva goal!'" she told *Billboard* in 2014.

But Ariana's whole career has been about setting "helluva goals" and surpassing them beyond anyone's expectations—except, perhaps, her own. While those initial meetings as a young teen didn't result in a record deal, by the time she released her debut album, the candy-coated love letter to '90s R&B and old-school doo-wop *Yours Truly*, she'd gained enough autonomy over her music career to kick it off in a fashion that, she said, felt true to her.

MUSIC FROM THE START

Music surrounded Ariana as a child. Her family held living-room karaoke sessions where she enjoyed the full range of their musical passions. Her mother, Joan Grande, loved big-voiced divas like Barbra Streisand and Céline Dion, while her dad, Edward Butera, was more of a Beatles fan. Her brother Frankie's selections, meanwhile, were "a mix of everything," Ari told *Fresh Air* in 2025, from late-twentieth-century pop icons like Spice Girls and Madonna to his cherished musical-theater icon Judy Garland.

Ariana found her own voice early on. Joan told *People* that Ariana belted out "one of JC [Chasez]'s power high notes" while the two were driving around listening to the hitmaking boy band *NSYNC. Ariana was only three and a half at the time, and her mother expressed amazement at her daughter's vocal power. Even at that age, Ariana was nonchalant about her talents. "She thought everybody sounded like that," Joan said.

ARIANA DEVELOPS HER TALENT

As Ariana developed her craft, singing in musical productions at home in Boca Raton and on Broadway as well as on her YouTube channel, she also figured out the kind of music she liked to make, producing songs on GarageBand that took cues from art-pop producer-vocalist Imogen Heap, an electropop pioneer whose songs like the striking 2005 cut "Hide and

RIGHT Ariana graces the red carpet at the 62nd Annual Grammy Awards in Los Angeles on January 26, 2020. After skipping the 2019 awards due to what Ariana characterized as artistic differences with the event producers, in 2020, she walked the red carpet twice, in two different dresses. (You can see the first dress on page 104.) Her second outfit of the evening featured a Schiaparelli gray satin crop top and full skirt. When asked why the switch, she simply said, "I had two very special custom looks made and I couldn't decide." Ariana also performed during the award ceremony.

Seek" were beloved for their intricate construction and multilayered vocals.

Ariana's range and power invited comparisons to Mariah Carey—a flattering resemblance because Carey was someone, Ariana told *Fresh Air*, she'd "looked up to . . . endlessly," alongside Whitney Houston and Dion. "I think that's a large part of the reason why I learned to sing, because that's who I was singing along with," she said.

As soon as her breakthrough single "The Way" came out in 2013, Ariana had carved out her own lane, blending her technical prowess and four-octave range with the broad yet razor-sharp knowledge of popular music she'd nurtured since childhood. The two factors, together, were unstoppable, and the big-name collaborators she worked with, from storied R&B producer Kenneth "Babyface" Edmonds to twenty-first-century hit machine Max Martin, took notice instantly. "What makes an Ariana song an Ariana song is that it's a song no one else can sing," Savan Kotecha, who co-wrote Ariana's playful hit "Problem," told *Billboard* in 2014. "She's probably one of [the best], if not the best, technical singers of her generation."

SHE STAYS CURIOUS

In addition to having extraordinary vocal ability, Ariana also has a restless urge to experiment and a boundless curiosity. That hunger for the new, combined with her already-impressive musical knowledge, consistently leads her to anticipate and further current pop trends. "Break Free," from 2014's *My Everything*, was a neon-lit collaboration with the EDM producer Zedd that showed Ari could command a modern-day dance floor. "Dangerous Woman," the title track of her third album, transported the storm and pomp of a James Bond theme to the twenty-first century; that same 2016 full-length album also included "Side to Side," a reggae-tinged team-up with red-hot Queens MC Nicki Minaj.

Over time, Ariana took more control in the studio and of her material. On 2018's *Sweetener*, she told podcaster Zach Sang, she mostly kept her vocal range in what she called "my sweet lower register," and also figured out how to make her vocals fit together in ways that showcased her ad-libs and vocal runs while giving the music sonic depth. "I did four million harmonies on everything," she said. "That's my favorite thing to do, is [to] vocal arrange." In recent years, she's released footage of herself in the studio to let fans in on her songs' progress and allow them to watch her figure out how each track of her voice can dart through the music for maximum impact. She typically records multiple takes of a single line, then "stacks" them on the finished product.

BUT THAT VOICE!

"I try to be very discerning with the ways I use my voice," Ariana told *Fresh Air* in 2025. "I try to find the right places and moments and make sure that it's with an emotional attachment or serving a purpose." Ariana was talking about employing her whistle register, the high-soprano range that she's used to great effect on songs like the slow-dancing trap-pop cut "Imagine" or the holly-jolly remix of whistle-note queen Mariah Carey's holiday jingle "Oh Santa!"

The discography she's amassed since 2013 feels both whole and compact, its flights of fancy to different genres and styles all remaining true to Ariana's vision while spinning in unexpected directions.

STAYING TRUE TO HER R&B ROOTS

Even though she's expanded her musical world into many genres, Ariana still feels a strong pull toward R&B. *Eternal Sunshine* in 2024 included "The Boy Is Mine," which combines feather-light sonics with Ariana's yearning voice and a stop-starting beat that heightens the dramatic tension of her attempts to reel in a potential lover. Before the album dropped, she told Apple Music's Zane Lowe that she'd been inspired by soul singers Brandy and Monica's 1998 duet of the same name, a blockbuster crossover hit by two young up-and-comers that defined late-nineties pop-R&B.

"I always wanted to reimagine that song in some kind of way," she said. A few months after *Eternal Sunshine* dropped, Ariana announced a "Boy" remix—one featuring none other than Brandy and Monica. "This is in celebration of you both and the impact that you have had on every vocalist, vocal producer, musician, artist that is creating today," Ariana wrote on Instagram when announcing the remix.

ARIANA KEEPS REACHING

Ariana's vision for her music has evolved over the years, but her central goals have rarely wavered—she's wanted to honor her natural talent and the artists who inspired her to embark on her own journey while exploring new creative frontiers. When she was a teenage singer hoping to break through with an R&B album, music executives said she had set a "helluva goal" for herself. Less than two decades later, she has not only reached and surpassed those goals, she's shown that—like her voice—she's always reaching ever-higher heights. 🦋

By Maura Johnston

'Dangerous Woman' is one of my favorite songs. I had to fight for it to be the first single. I said, 'This will fulfill me. This is what I want to say right now. I'm coming into my own, I'm trusting myself.' It was kind of a personal anthem saying that girls can do whatever they want."

–ARIANA TO *COSMOPOLITAN* IN MARCH 2017

Ariana 360
THE PONYTAIL

HER PERSONAL STYLE has shifted through the years, but there is one iconic element that fans can always count on: Ariana's tight, sweeping updo. She first adopted the style because her hair was damaged after bleaching and dying it red to play Cat Valentine, but then it became a way to communicate how she was feeling. Hair stylist Chris Appleton, who worked with Ariana in 2018, revealed that the height of her ponytail is like a mood ring. "It's all about the placement," he said to *Teen Vogue*. "The higher you go, the fiercer it looks."

A TRESSES TIMELINE
• The ponytail debuted as a curly half-up, half-down style in 2013.

• From 2014 to 2016, her hair became blonder as the pony's angle got higher.

• Starting in 2016, the ponytail was generally worn straight, and Ariana also experimented with bangs. Into 2018, the ponytail was often dark as well as straight.

2013

2014

2016

2018

2018

2020

2020

2025

• At the 2018 Met Gala, Ariana dressed up the pony with a huge, floppy bow that resembled a nun's headpiece to fit that year's theme, "Heavenly Bodies: Fashion and the Catholic Imagination" (see more of her look on page 57).

• During pandemic lockdowns, Ari showcased her natural hair in a more casual look. But during a performance with Lady Gaga at the MTV Video Music Awards, the ponytail became pigtails.

• Taking the role of Galinda in *Wicked* led to her dyeing her hair blond—but the ponytail still made frequent appearances during the movie's press tour in 2025.

• The cover of *Eternal Sunshine: Brighter Days Ahead*, which came out in March 2025, shows her suspended in midair, her ponytail floating. Her pony is Glinda-blond in the music video for the album's second single, "We Can't Be Friends (Wait for Your Love)" (see page 108).

TOP In January 2002, at just eight years old, Ariana made her first solo public appearance when she sang "The Star-Spangled Banner" at a Florida Panthers game. In a 2020 appearance on *The Tonight Show Starring Jimmy Fallon*, Ariana called the performance "her first big gig."

BOTTOM Ariana performs "A Brand New You" with the cast of *13* at the 17th Broadway on Broadway event in September 2008. Refinery29 calls the song "a hit for the ages." During the show, she formed a friendship with composer and lyricist Jason Robert Brown, and the two have collaborated since. In 2013, he wrote a song with her—"Jason's Song (Gave It Away)." Brown said "you only need to spend about two minutes in Ari's company to recognize what an amazing musician and what a total pro she is."

FAR RIGHT Ariana and Justin Bieber first perform on the same stage at *Variety*'s annual Power of Youth event on October 24, 2010, in Hollywood. The two would go on to become close friends and collaborators.

Backstage during her Listening Sessions tour in August 2013, Ariana holds a platinum record celebrating one million copies sold of her single "The Way," featuring Malcolm "Mac" Miller. The song was released in March 2013 and quickly became a hit.

> **"I love her. I think she's amazing. . . . She's super talented, and working together was really fun."**
>
> —MARIAH CAREY TO *PEOPLE*, DECEMBER 23, 2024

LEFT Opting for a medley of "The Way" and "Baby I," Ariana sings during the preshow for the 2013 MTV Video Music Awards at the Barclays Center in Brooklyn. She later tweeted "Maybe I can stop shaking now. That was so much fun . . . Thank u for the love hope u enjoyed!"

RIGHT Ariana and Nathan Sykes of the English boy band the Wanted arrive at the BBC in London on October 11, 2013. The two met when they collaborated on her song "Almost Is Never Enough" on *Yours Truly*. As their relationship evolved from collaborators to romantic partners, Ariana experienced her first relationship in the limelight—fans even dubbed the couple "Nariana." The love affair didn't last long; by December 2013 they had called it quits citing distance as the main factor.

LEFT It all started with a tweet. When Ariana asked her fans what they were thankful for on Thanksgiving 2012, Pittsburgh rapper, producer, and songwriter Mac Miller replied—from there, the two continued talking, becoming collaborators, friends, and eventually partners. In 2013, Ari heard "The Way" from producer Harry Samuels and instantly knew Mac would be the perfect addition. Ariana said their music video, released in March 2013, was the "most fun" to make, telling *Teen Vogue*, "We had no budget, didn't even tell the label that we were gonna do it . . . [we] made it ourselves."

RIGHT Ariana and Iggy Azalea present the Moonman for Best Male Artist to Justin Bieber at the 2013 MTV European Music Awards held at the Ziggo Dome in Amsterdam, Netherlands, on November 10, 2013. According to Ariana, the two women "hit it off" at the award show, and went on to make the song "Problem" from *My Everything* together.

[P]eople are so much more capable and can do so much more than what their quote-unquote identity has them listed as. If you give her any canvas to paint on she's going to paint a very beautiful picture."

–MAC MILLER TO *ROLLING STONE*, SEPTEMBER 20, 2016

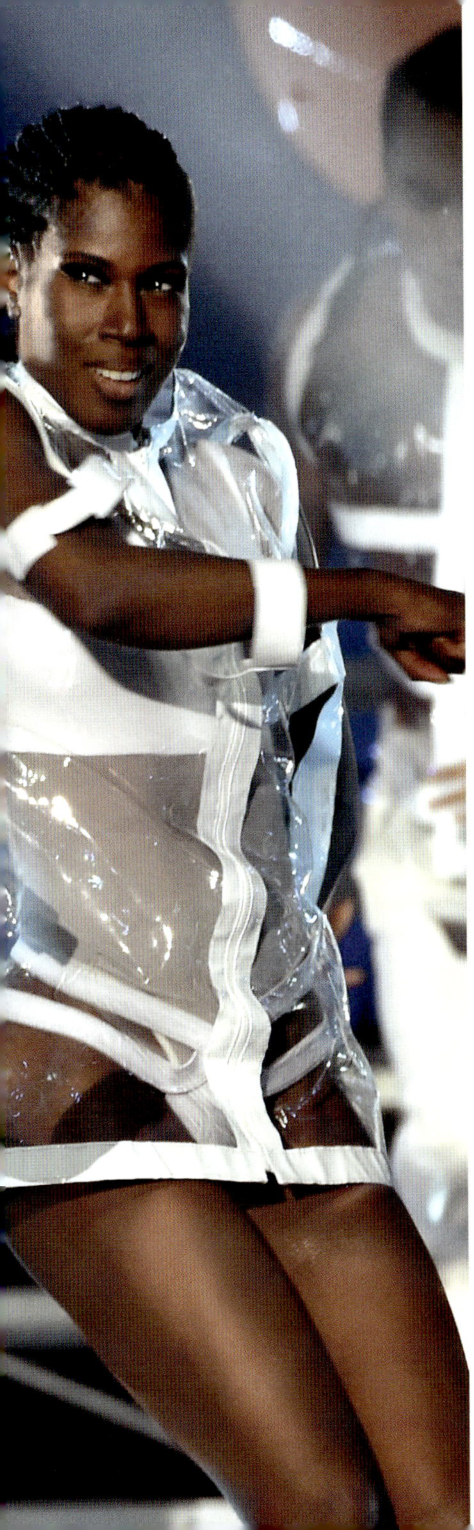

LEFT Ariana opened the 2014 MTV Video Music Awards at the Forum in Inglewood, California, on August 24, with a dazzling performance of her EDM hit "Break Free" from *My Everything*.

RIGHT Ariana poses at the award show. That night she snagged her first Moonman—the MTV Video Music Award for best pop video. Her '60s throwback video for "Problem" beat out Pharrell, John Legend, and others for the win—including Iggy Azalea, who collaborated with Ariana on the winner. Jim Carrey presented Ariana with the Moonman.

My point of view as a producer and as a writer, if she's not comfortable, she's never going to give me the pure her. . . . Not a lot of people let all of that out. They want to work behind the confines of their cool or what they feel comfortable with. This record, she really unzipped."

–PHARRELL WILLIAMS ON WORKING WITH ARIANA ON *SWEETENER* TO ZACH SANG, AUGUST 17, 2018

RIGHT Ariana, Nicki Minaj (left), and English singer Jessie J (center) perform at the American Music Awards at the Nokia Theatre on November 23, 2014. Their song "Bang Bang" appeared on both Jessie J's album *Sweet Talker* and the deluxe version of *My Everything*. In 2024, the track was certified diamond by the Recording Industry Association of America for selling more than 10 million copies and becoming the first collaboration by women in the history of the RIAA to achieve that milestone.

LEFT Ariana and Detroit MC Big Sean grin at each other as they perform during KIIS FM's Jingle Ball in December 2014. The two first crossed paths when he contributed a verse to her song "Right There" on *Yours Truly*. The two were reunited on *My Everything*, performing the moody "Best Mistake." Not long after, the pair's relationship went from professional to romantic.

ABOVE Ariana debuts on the Grammys stage on February 8, 2015, in Los Angeles, performing "Just a Little Bit of Your Heart." The song, co-written by Harry Styles, shows off Ariana's voice—especially her high notes. A twelve-person string section and a piano accompanied her.

R&B singer Babyface and Ariana perform the Steve Wonder classic "Signed, Sealed, Delivered (I'm Yours)" at the February 10, 2015, tribute *Songs in the Key of Life— An All-Star Grammy Salute*. Babyface also worked with Ariana on *Yours Truly* and *Christmas Kisses*, producing and composing several songs.

"
I love her voice.
Her tone is
golden and it just
feels good.
She's got one of
those feel-good
voices we
haven't heard in
a long time."

–KENNETH "BABYFACE"
EDMONDS TO *COMPLEX*, 2013

Ariana sports cat ears for her Honeymoon Tour stop at the Lanxess Arena on June 13, 2015, in Cologne, Germany. She started wearing the ears for Halloween when she dressed up as a cat. "I always am a cat for Halloween," she told Power 106 FM in 2014.

" It turns out that under the surface, Grande is gloriously weird at heart— watching her now is like the scene in the horror movie where the prom queen whips out an ax."

–ROB SHEFFIELD IN *ROLLING STONE*, JANUARY 11, 2019

LEFT Ariana accepts the Artist of the Year award at the 2016 American Music Awards. During her speech at the November 20 event in Los Angeles, she thanked her fans. "I think of you with everything I do. You guys are everything to me."

RIGHT Ariana and Nicki Minaj join forces again on the reggae-tinged "Side to Side," from Ariana's third album, *Dangerous Woman*. Released as a single in August 2016, the song peaked at No. 4 on the Hot 100. The duo poses during a performance of the track at the 2016 MTV Video Music Awards at Madison Square Garden.

PAGE 90-91 Ari sings during the sweat-soaked, spin-class-themed performance of "Side to Side" at the 2016 VMAs. MTV News observed that, in the song, Minaj is "rapping about something a bit more risque than your standard gym workout."

LEFT Waving a Pride flag, Ariana performs at the iHeartRadio concert on June 2, 2018, at the Bank of America stadium in Los Angeles. She previews songs, including "The Light Is Coming," from her fourth studio album, *Sweetener*, released later that summer.

RIGHT (TOP AND BOTTOM) Ariana wins a Moonman for Best Pop Video for "No Tears Left to Cry" at the 2018 MTV Video Music Awards on August 20 at Radio City Music Hall in New York City. After thanking fans, family, and colleagues, she adds, "Pete Davidson, thanks for existing." Later that night, in the audience at the event, the *SNL* actor and comedian holds Ariana's hand. The pair started dating in May that year, after Ariana's breakup with Mac Miller, and got engaged shortly after. They broke up by October.

LEFT Ariana kicks off a series of small, intimate concerts—the first being at Irving Plaza in New York City on August 20, 2018, immediately after her appearance at the MTV Video Music Awards. The concerts, called the Sweetener Sessions, are held over eighteen days following the album's release. After New York, she performed in Chicago, Los Angeles, and London.

RIGHT Ariana begins the Sweetener World Tour on March 18, 2019, at the Times Union Center in Albany, New York. Before she takes the stage there's a tribute to Mac Miller, who had died in September 2018 from an accidental overdose: The preshow soundtrack included Miller's song "Dang."

The R&B legend known as the Godmother of Soul, Patti LaBelle, presents Ariana with *Billboard*'s Woman of the Year award in December 2018. The two had met years earlier in 2014 when they performed at the Women of Soul concert hosted at the White House by President Barack Obama and First Lady Michelle Obama. At the *Billboard* ceremony, held at Pier 36 in New York, LaBelle says Ariana is "soulful, strong, and she's just sensational—she's all that and a bag of chips."

> # "
> ### She's a baby who's able to sing like an older black woman. . . . Ariana can sing me under the table— and listen, I can sing."
>
> **–PATTI LABELLE TO *VOGUE*, JULY 9, 2019**

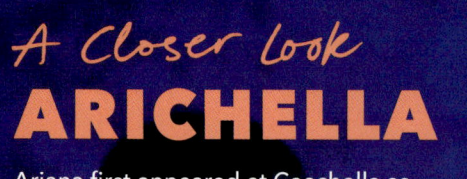

A Closer Look
ARICHELLA

Ariana first appeared at Coachella as a surprise guest during Norwegian DJ Kygo's 2018 set, singing "No More Tears Left to Cry" and a cover of Marvin Gaye's "Sexual Healing."

In 2019, Ariana returned to headline Sunday on both weekends of the Southern California music festival, which fans renamed Arichella.

Ariana dazzles festival audiences. Her show-stopping set includes multiple costume changes, killer dance moves, and special guests. On the first weekend of the festival on April 14, 2019, Ariana brought out Nicki Minaj and *NSYNC and proclaimed to the crowd, "I've been practicing my whole life for this moment! I could die now!"

After trilling the beautiful notes of "Raindrops (An Angel Cried)," Ariana opens her second Coachella set, on April 21, 2019, with "God Is a Woman." The BBC wrote "This was all Grande: the hits, the hair, the voice, and that personality we've come to adore."

ABOVE Ariana and *NSYNC (minus Justin Timberlake) pose backstage at Coachella. She brought out her childhood heroes during "Break Up with Your Girlfriend, I'm Bored," which samples their song "It Makes Me Ill," and they stayed onstage to perform "Tearin' Up My Heart."

LEFT AND ABOVE Arichella features fabulous fashion. For both weekends of Coachella, Ariana wore four different costumes, a purple bralette with puffed shoulders and skirt (above and right) designed by Michael Ngo, a lilac-colored buckled bralette with tiered skirt and frilly sleeves (left), a ruby-colored sequin bralette and short skirt, and a similar look in bubblegum pink. All were accessorized with Ariana's signature over-the-knee stiletto boots and high ponytail.

RIGHT Nicki Minaj is a surprise performer at Arichella, joining Ariana for "Bang, Bang" and "Side to Side" during the first weekend. Unfortunately, technical issues with the sound frustrate the friends, but they shrug it off.

ABOVE Ariana went through a succession of costume changes at the 2020 Grammys. Here she shows off the first dress of the night: a gray tiered tulle confection designed by Giambattista Valli.

RIGHT At the same show, Ariana performs a medley of her song "Imagine" and "My Favorite Things" from *The Sound of Music* before segueing into the Rodgers and Hammerstein-sampled "7 Rings" (see her next look on page 2).

> **When life tries you with such serious shit so many times, your priorities change . . . I just want to be happy and healthy—one day—and make music."**
>
> —ARIANA TO *BILLBOARD*,
> DECEMBER 5, 2018

ABOVE A charity single, "Stuck with U" was released in May 2020, with the net proceeds going to support the First Responders Children's Foundation. An official video for the song features a montage of videos of people isolating at home, including Ariana snuggling with her dog Toulouse.

LEFT Ariana makes a cameo during Lady Gaga's 2020 MTV Video Music Awards performance, a medley of *Chromatica* tracks including "Rain on Me," wearing a mask and moon boots. Released on May 22 during the COVID shutdowns, the song was a stomping, glossy house track featuring Gaga and Ariana singing triumphantly about how the hard times they've endured make them stronger. The No. 1 hit became one of the defining tracks of the pandemic summer and won Song of the Year at the 2020 VMAs, one of four awards Ariana received that night.

ABOVE (TOP AND BOTTOM) Ariana released *Positions* on October 30, 2020, and wasn't able to tour because of concerns about COVID. In the video for the album's title track, Ariana takes on a number of roles in the White House.

ABOVE (TOP AND BOTTOM) Ariana appears in the video for "We Can't Be Friends (Wait for Your Love)." The song was the second single from *Eternal Sunshine*, Ariana's seventh studio album, released on March 8, 2024.

Positions **searches for peace, tracing the quiet work of piecing yourself together and delighting in giddy new romance at the same time."**

–DANI BLUM, *PITCHFORK*, NOVEMBER 2, 2020

Ariana performs several songs from *Eternal Sunshine* live for the first time at the 2024 Met Gala including "The Boy Is Mine" and "Yes, And?"

Ariana 360

THE COLLABORATOR

ARIANA HAS ALWAYS worked closely with other singers, connecting with them on professional and personal levels. Ari and the R&B singer the Weeknd first collaborated on the plush *My Everything* cut "Love Me Harder" in 2014, and by the 2020s they'd become regulars on each other's albums, with the Weeknd guesting on *Positions*' "Off the Table" and Ariana hopping in on two Weeknd remixes, the melancholic "Save Your Tears" and the dreamy "Die for You," in 2021 and 2023. Both those remixes went to No. 1 on the Hot 100.

Fast-talking Queens MC Nicki Minaj met Ariana for the

first time in 2011, when Minaj was bathing in the glow of her debut album *Pink Friday* and Ari was beginning to figure out her pop career. Since then, Minaj has become Ari's most frequent collaborator, with tracks like the boisterous "Bang Bang" (which also featured British belter Jessie J) and the sinuous "Side to Side" becoming summer hits in the 2010s, and the spaced-out 2018 collab "The Light Is Coming" showing how Ari's vision of pop had evolved in a short period of time.

In 2011, teen pop star Justin Bieber visited the set of *Victorious*, answering questions posed by the cast during Nickelodeon's "Crush Week." Ariana asked, "What inspires your music more—being happy in love, or heartbreak?" That question, which sparked a lively discussion about songwriting, kicked off a fruitful creative partnership between the two. Only a few years later, Ariana opened a handful of dates on Bieber's Believe Tour, and two years after that, Bieber joined Ariana onstage during the Honeymoon Tour's Miami stop, singing his hit "As Long as You Love Me" and duetting with her on "Love Me Harder." In the fall of 2015, they released their first on-record collab, a remix

LEFT At the 2014 AMAs on November 23, Ariana and Canadian singer the Weeknd perform "Love Me Harder" from Ariana's album *My Everything*. The friends have collaborated on six songs, four of which have been publicly released.

ABOVE Ariana and Nicki Minaj smile onstage at the November 2016 American Music Awards in Los Angeles. Ariana said of Minaj before the show, "I love Nicki; this is the third song we've done together, and this is one of my favorite songs on the album."

of Bieber's pumping *Purpose* track "What Do You Mean?" Bieber performed at One Love Manchester in 2018 and joined Ari onstage at the second weekend of Arichella the next year; in 2020 they joined forces for the sweetly romantic "Stuck with U," and the song, propelled by its lockdown-themed video, gave them their first joint No. 1 single.

Singer-songwriter Victoria Monét met Ariana in 2013, and the two quickly bonded over their shared love of R&B. Monét racked up co-writing credits on every one of Ariana's albums through 2020's *Positions*.

Ari's 2020 collaboration with larger-than-life art-pop star Lady Gaga, "Rain on Me," became one of the pandemic era's defining hits, its message of triumphing over trauma and lightning-bolt synths turning home lockdowns into dance floors. The singers forged an immediate bond.

And of course there's the connection between Ariana and her *Wicked* co-star Cynthia Erivo. The two seemed inseparable as they promoted the film. The actresses met in 2021 at Erivo's house and talked for hours. "I think we found a little piece of ourselves in each other," Erivo told *Cosmopolitan*.

ABOVE Victoria Monét and Ariana sing "Better Days" at One Love Manchester in June 2017. The song, a collaboration originally released on Monét's SoundCloud after several 2016 police-involved shootings as well as police deaths during a protest in Dallas, calls for a stop to violence.

TOP RIGHT Lady Gaga and Ariana attend *Stevie Wonder: Songs in the Key of Life–An All-Star Grammy Salute* at the Nokia Theatre on February 10, 2015.

BOTTOM RIGHT Ariana closes her surprise performance at the 2024 Met Gala with a duet of "When You Believe" with Cynthia Erivo. In an Instagram post after the event, Ariana thanked her *Wicked* co-star "for lighting up the museum brighter than any star in the sky ever could."

The 97th Academy Awards in March 2025 brings Ariana's worlds together in one triumphant night. Nominated for Best Supporting Actress, she was also one of the event's lead performers. She opened the night singing "Over the Rainbow," a song that has become closely associated with the singer after she closed One Love Manchester with it.

THE CULTURAL PHENOM

Ariana Grande Is Here to Save Us

What special alchemy transforms a pop star into a true cultural phenomenon who transcends their music to become a global icon? In the case of Ariana Grande, it seems to be a steady light that burns within, keeping her focused on her mission.

But what kindles that light and keeps it glowing, especially when challenges arise? *Elle* writer Katie Connor captured some of what makes Ariana *Ariana* in their 2018 conversation.

Ariana Grande is a star. A really big star. For millions of Arianators, as her fans are known, she's a radiant, life-giving force they wake up with in the morning and go to bed with at night.

Calling to them is Ariana's honeyed, four-octave voice. But they're also drawn to her sparkle: The poofy lampshade and figure skater–style dresses. The cat, bunny, and Minnie Mouse ears she wears often and without ceremony. On social media, she speaks to her fans in fluent internet, playing fast and loose with a "see no evil" monkey emoji and crafting full sentences in acronyms only. And then, of course, there's her signature Vegas-fountain ponytail, the orientation, height, and shade of which Arianators track like an ancient civilization charting the moon. To the casual observer,

the singer's idiosyncrasies might seem juvenile, absurd even, but there's a subversiveness to Ariana's child's play. Her bright and shiny optics belie a far more nuanced character. She's been in therapy for more than ten years, since around the time her parents divorced, and thus traffics in self-awareness. "It's work," she tells me, sitting on the couch in her hotel suite overlooking Central Park. "I've also spent the past handful of years growing up under very extraordinary circumstances. And I know how that story goes." Cut to former child star in a mug shot. And scene.

She speaks of the strength of community in this "tough, wild, chaotic time right now" and considers just how divided the nation is. Her call to action: "Everyone has to have uncomfortable conversations with their relatives. Instead of unfriending people on Facebook who share different political views, comment! Have a conversation! Try to spread the fucking light." She's become something of a feminist hero for her ability to shut down sexism and misogyny with a single tweet. One, in 2018, regarded her ex, rapper Mac Miller, who allegedly drove drunk and crashed his car shortly after their breakup. A Twitter user suggested it was Ariana's fault. "How absurd that you minimize female self-respect and self-worth by saying someone should stay in a toxic relationship," she wrote. "Shaming/blaming women for a man's inability to keep his shit together is a very major problem . . . please stop doing that." The user apologized. She accepted. [Mac Miller passed away not long after this interview, and Ariana has consistently both honored his memory and acknowledged the pain that loving someone with profound mental health or addiction challenges poses in a way that is very Ariana.]

A sly, mischievous streak runs through Ariana's maternal bloodline. "It's the Italian thing; we have the dark humor," she says. Her mother Joan is a soft-spoken firebrand. The Brooklyn-born, Barnard-educated woman was "goth before goth was goth," she says, and name-checks Poe and Hawthorne as favored college companions. At home in Boca Raton, Florida, she made the macabre fun for Ariana and her brother, Frankie. Halloween was as big of a deal

as Christmas. "I did the house up in things that would give normal children nightmares," she says. "I would go to the butcher, get heart organs or lungs, and then be like, 'Ariana, Frankie, this is a heart.' The kids would paint blood on the walls. I remember Ariana's little handprints."

The family went to Disney World pretty regularly, where Ariana was drawn to baddies like Cruella de Vil and Maleficent. "If we had a choice of going to the Disney princess store or the villain store, it was always the villains," Joan says. It's worth noting that the biggest fights between mother and daughter "had to do with boys."

There's a bouquet of white roses on the coffee table in Ariana's hotel. The note: "To my darling Ariana: You are the true work of art! Love you dearly, Mommy." It's been almost a year since they fled a UK terrorist attack that claimed twenty-two lives, injuring five hundred more, at the sold-out Manchester show of Ariana's Dangerous Woman Tour. Ariana is hesitant to talk about it. For one thing, the wound is still incredibly raw, but she's also adamant that her story not overshadow those of the victims. So we talk around it. "When I got home from tour, I had really wild dizzy spells, this feeling like I couldn't breathe," she begins. "I would be in a good mood, fine and happy, and they would hit me out of nowhere. I've always had anxiety, but it had never been physical before. There were a couple of months straight where I felt so upside down." She shared the experience with her friend Pharrell

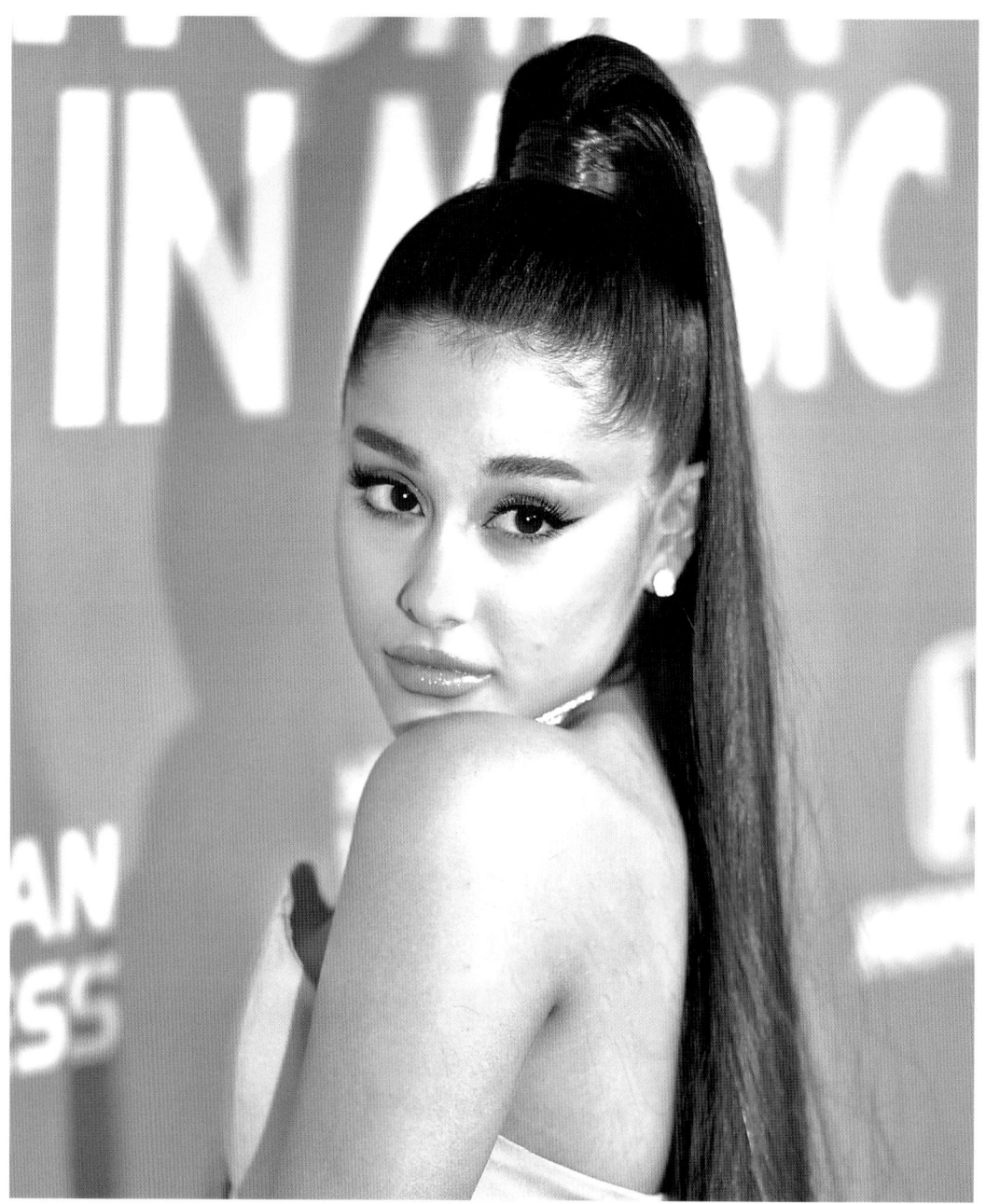

Williams. Together they created "Get Well Soon," the final track on *Sweetener*.

"It's all the voices in my head talking to one another," she explains, before softly serenading me. "'They say my system is overloaded,'" she sings, "and then the background vocals say, 'Girl, what's wrong with you? Come back down.'" The studio version is a veritable mille-feuille of vocal arrangement, stacking layers upon layers of Ariana's voice until she lands, wholly, right side up.

On how the event has changed Ariana, Joan says, "She loves a bit more fearlessly than she did before." I gently broach the subject with Ariana, and the name "Manchester" alone triggers a huge teardrop to roll down her cheek. "You hear about these things," she starts slowly. "You see it on the news, you tweet the hashtag. It's happened before, and it'll happen again. It makes you sad, you think about it for a little, and then people move on. But experiencing something like that firsthand, you think of everything differently." She pauses, swallowing the lump in her throat. "Everything is different." Getting back onstage was "terrifying." It still is sometimes. She credits her fans as being her primary source of courage. "It's the most inspiring thing in the world that these kids pack the venue. They're smiling, holding signs saying, 'Hate will never win.'" The tears are full-on now. "Why would I second-guess getting on a fucking stage and being there for them? That city, and their response? That changed my life."

She'd go on to complete the rest of her world tour, capping it off with a performance at a Concert for Charlottesville, another city reeling in the aftermath of senseless violence. A lot of mainstream top 40 types are seemingly reluctant to take a political stance. The fear being, presumably, a loss of fan base and revenue. "That's wild to me," Ariana says. She is loud and proud in her anti-Trumpism and has aligned herself with gun reform and Black Lives Matter. I wonder if she's gotten any backlash. "Of course!" she says. "There's a lot of noise when you say anything about anything. But if I'm not going to say it, what's the fucking point of being here? Not everyone is going to agree with you, but that doesn't mean I'm just going to shut up and sing my songs. I'm also going to be a human being who cares about other human beings; to be an ally and use my privilege to help educate people." For her, the role of the artist is to "not only help people and comfort them, but also push people to think differently, raise questions, and push their boundaries mentally."

I think of a song on *Sweetener* that I had misjudged based on the title alone. I assume "The Light Is Coming" will be a sweet balm of a ballad in response to the darkest of days. Nope. It's a bass-thumping dance track featuring Ariana's friend, collaborator, and "big sis," Nicki Minaj. "The light is coming to give back everything the darkness stole," Ariana trills. But then, what is light without the dark? 🦋

By Katie Connor for Elle, *2018*

121

Ariana 360

THE ENTREPRENEUR

BEYOND HER TRIUMPHS as a musician and actor, Ariana has also had astounding success as a businessperson. In 2015 Ariana launched Ari by Ariana Grande, her first fragrance, and she promoted it by toting around a giant replica of its pink crystal bottle on *Good Morning America* and handing out samples to attendees of the Honeymoon Tour in Toronto. Since then, she's released a slew of fragrances, each in a signature sculptured bottle that's pure Ariana, and has sold more than $1 billion worth of product. Her perfume line has punched well above the typical celebrity fragrance, winning awards and setting a new standard for celebrity offerings.

Not one to be limited to just one direction, in November 2021, Ari launched r.e.m. beauty, a cruelty-free line of eye, lip, and face makeup that, she told *Elle*, she'd road tested personally. Since then, she's expanded the line, adding skincare products,

concealers, and foundations named after *Sweetener*, and a line honoring *Wicked*. Its latest batch of new products, the Dreamglow Collection, features r.e.m.'s products in shimmering colors. The company grossed $88.7 million in 2023, according to the marketing agency Upbeat.

In addition to launching her own products, Ariana has collaborated with major brands. In 2019, Starbucks honored Ariana and her oft-used cloud imagery on social media with the Cloud Macchiato. (Ariana, a vegan, suggested that her fans try the soy version.) The Cloud Macchiato's launch reportedly boosted Starbucks' sales that quarter, with then-CEO Kevin Johnson calling the Ari-Starbucks synergy "the second most viral Starbucks campaign ever." Ari has also partnered with the cosmetic company MAC on its lip line Viva Glam (which originally supported the MAC AIDS Fund, a charity that supports people

living with HIV and AIDS), American Express (which sponsored her Sweetener Sessions mini-tour), and the crystal company Swarovski (which named her their brand ambassador in 2024).

Ariana strikes a pose in front of a poster for MAC Viva Glam cosmetics in 2016. The proceeds from Viva Glam support a range of LGBTQIA+ charities, as well as health and climate initiatives. The fund has raised over $534 million since its start.

TOP LEFT In November 2024 a Sunset Boulevard billboard advertises Ariana as the new face of Swarovski. The crystal company says of their brand ambassador, "an advocate for inclusivity and empowerment, she is the epitome of joyful extravagance and self-expression."

TOP RIGHT Blending her businesses, Ariana's fragrance God Is a Woman is made available to guests in the gift lounge at iHeartRadio Z100 Jingle Ball 2021 in New York. The fragrance line is known for its signature architectural bottles with both fragrance names and containers often nodding to her songs.

LEFT Ariana unveils her debut fragrance, Ari by Ariana Grande, in New York at Macy's Herald Square on September 16, 2015. While this first scent did not blow away experts, since then the beauty entrepreneur has only improved the quality of the fragrances. With more than fourteen fragrances distinguished by their "playful sweetness," Ariana has built the line into a billion-dollar business.

A Closer Look

THE ADVOCATE & ALLY

Following the terrorist bombing in Manchester, Ariana experienced anxiety attacks during the rest of the Dangerous Woman Tour. The death of her longtime collaborator Mac Miller the next year took an additional toll. Struggling during these years, Ariana turned to music, channeling her emotions to create the 2018 album *Sweetener*. In addition to being open about her own mental health, Ariana also uses her energy and her platform to support others.

TOP RIGHT Ariana credits producer Pharrell Williams with helping her to translate her struggles into music when he produced *Sweetener*. Here, they attend the Grammy Awards on January 26, 2014, in Los Angeles.

RIGHT INSET Mac Miller and Ariana hold hands at an Oscar party on March 4, 2018, in Los Angeles, shortly before their breakup. Miller died by an accidental overdose several months after, and Ariana later acknowledged that his death compounded the mental health challenges she'd wrestled with since the Manchester attack.

FAR RIGHT Ariana has a reflective moment onstage during her Sweetener World Tour stop at Staples Center in Los Angeles on May 7, 2019. The pop star has been candid about the toll that touring and performing takes on her mental health, often writing about the subject on social media. In an April 2019 tweet, she wrote of her music, "Making it is healing. Performing it is like reliving it all over again and it is hell."

> ## "
> [Ariana] was forced to grow up in public with a tragedy: the terrorist bombing at her 2017 concert in Manchester, England."
>
> ROB SHEFFIELD, *ROLLING STONE*, JANUARY 11, 2019

ONE L♥VE MANCHES

> **" From the depraved dregs of humanity; the glorious blossoming of hope, a tangible act of togetherness; the salvation of pop. . . . Last night, Grande displayed leadership and charisma that the prime minister could only stiffly dream of."**
>
> **–HANNAH JANE PARKISON,**
> *THE GUARDIAN,* JUNE 5, 2017

Ariana sings during the One Love Manchester benefit concert at Old Trafford Cricket Ground on June 4, 2017. The benefit was held just two weeks after the terrorist attack, and all proceeds went to support victims and their families. The event included stars like Justin Bieber, Robbie Williams, Miley Cyrus, and Katy Perry; Ariana's friends and collaborators like Mac Miller and Imogen Heap; and Manchester royalty including Liam Gallagher of Oasis and David Beckham of Manchester United Football Club.

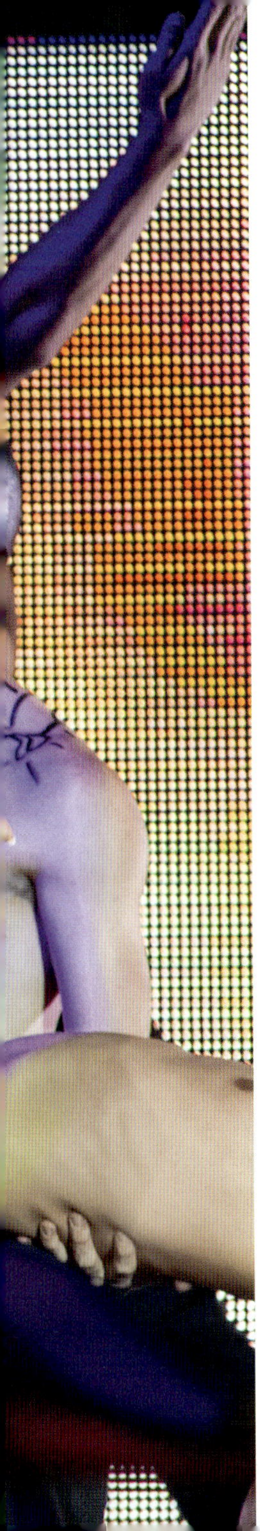

LEFT Ariana performs to an enthusiastic audience at NYC Pride: Dance on the Pier on June 28, 2015. She started her set with Whitney Houston's "I'm Every Woman" and Madonna's "Vogue" before segueing into "Problem," "Love Me Harder," "Bang Bang," and "Break Free."

LEFT Frankie Grande and Ariana attend Republic Records private post-VMA celebration at Ysabel on August 30, 2015, in West Hollywood. Of his sister, Frankie says, "She was raised in a family where gay was not only accepted, it was celebrated."

Ariana waves a Pride flag while she performs during the 2018 iHeartRadio Wango Tango by AT&T at Banc of California Stadium on June 2, 2018, in Los Angeles.

Reaching Oz

Ariana plays to the light and dark, finding strength and depth from personal experiences for her role of a lifetime.

**W**icked plays with themes of light and dark and also shades of gray. While at the surface, Glinda the Good Witch, played to pitch-perfect distinction by Ariana, is all pink bubbles and sunshine, if you look deeper, you'll find something more substantial.

During a panel at the Palm Springs International Film Festival, Ariana talked about the depth she found in her character:

"'No One Mourns the Wicked' is kind of a particularly complicated song. [Glinda] has to put on a strong face and provide hope and be a source of light for these strangers, essentially. She doesn't know them, but she loves them, and they love her. They're looking to her for this hope when she's also needing to find her own strength for herself, so it's kind of difficult."

In the same way that Ariana drew hope and inspiration from her relationship with her fans, she saw Glinda doing the same with the people of Oz. "I feel like sometimes in my professional life, I've had to perform through moments that felt tricky in that way," says Ariana, reflecting that her relationship with her fans is like Glinda and the Ozian's relationship too. "That same hope that they look to her for and that same void that they look to Glinda the Good to fill" feels reminiscent of her interaction with fans—that and they "feel it for her too when she's hurting."

Ariana's exceptional vocals made her a star, but her empathy, unwavering ideals, and ability to speak to real people about real issues have elevated her to true cultural phenomenon. Yes, she will give the finger to the patriarchy—female symbol tattooed on her middle finger for added emphasis—but she will also turn the outrage into joy, the pain into humor, and her real-life learnings into lessons for all of us. It's her realness and that indefinable ability to use pain to create joy that make her an icon.

As Ariana put it, again talking about *Wicked*, "It's the unexpected ways, the unexpected turns that my life has taken along the way that prepared me for Glinda way more than just loving pink and high notes and sparkles. It was the other stuff, the not-so-easy stuff, that I think I was able to use most for her because there's a lot underneath the surface."

RIGHT Ariana poses in a dress designed by Balenciaga's Demna for their fall 2023 couture collection. The look "balances elegance and cool," according to *Vogue*.

Co-stars Cynthia Erivo and Ariana and director Jon M. Chu work on the set of *Wicked* in 2024. The stars chose to sing their parts live on set rather than recording them in a studio. "It meant we would be further connected to the words we were saying and to each other," says Erivo. "There's something special about when music is live in a room."

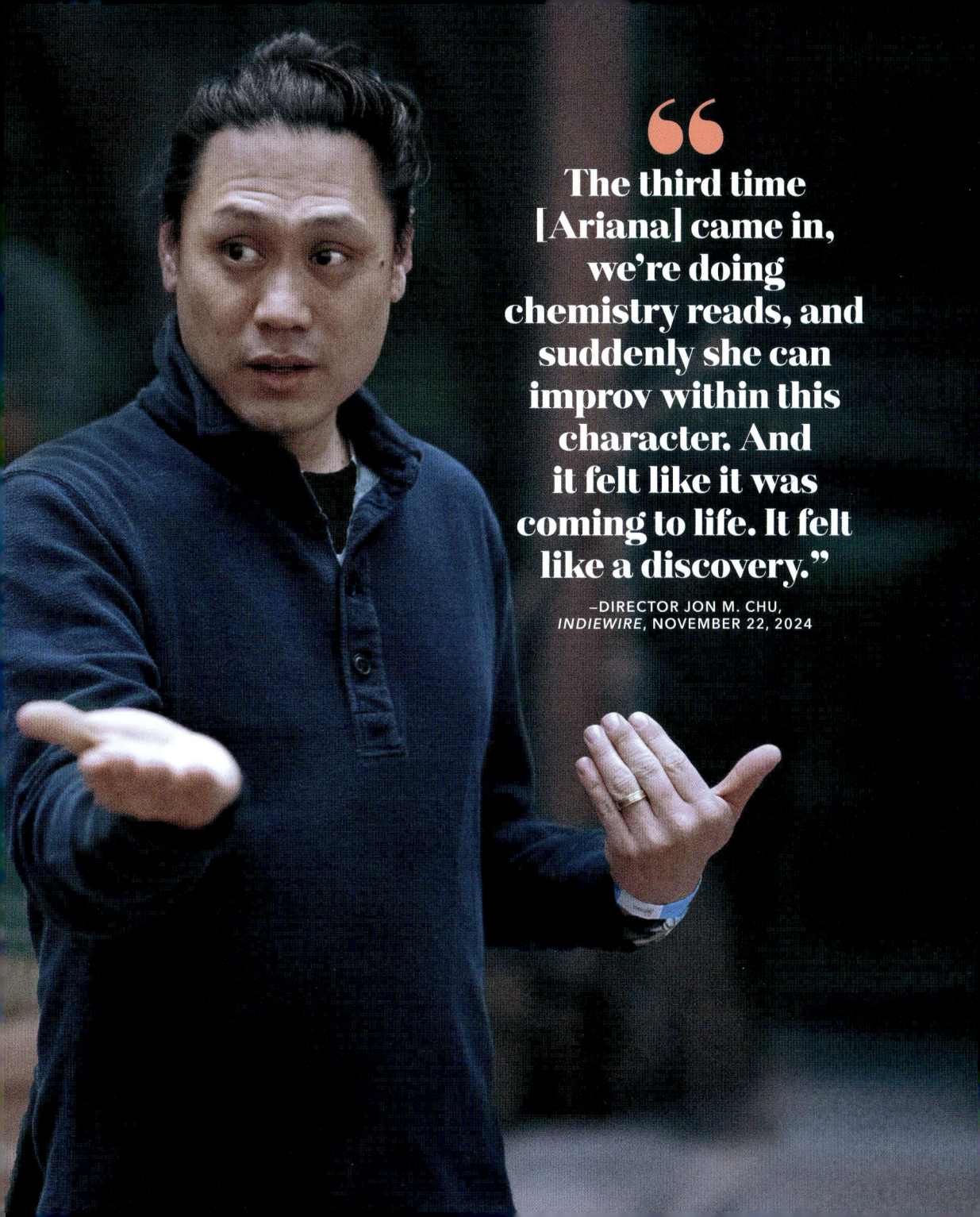

> **The third time [Ariana] came in, we're doing chemistry reads, and suddenly she can improv within this character. And it felt like it was coming to life. It felt like a discovery."**
>
> —DIRECTOR JON M. CHU,
> *INDIEWIRE*, NOVEMBER 22, 2024

LEFT Ariana arrives for the 2024 Met Gala at the Metropolitan Museum of Art. She conveyed the theme "Sleeping Beauties: Reawakening Fashion" through multiple ensembles and beauty choices, like 3-D fairy wings at her temples, designed by her makeup artist, Michael Anthony.

RIGHT For her first "look" of the evening, Ariana shines in a mother-of-pearl dress by Jonathan Anderson at Loewe that she said both reflected *Wicked* and had a personal connection—pearl is her birthstone. "I loved the tie-in of the opalescence and little hues of pink and green for Glinda's bubble and for *Wicked*," she said. "Pearls are just made in the most unexpected of ways. You never know what beautiful things you will find in unexpected places." Her co-star Cynthia Erivo is equally enchanting in custom Thom Browne.

Ariana sings at the 2024 Met Gala in a green tulle ensemble that glitters with rosettes, crystal embroidery, and gold dust. She began her surprise performance with "Once Upon a Dream" and a set of her solo hits before her *Wicked* co-star Cynthia Erivo joined her onstage. The two sang the Mariah Carey–Whitney Houston classic duet, "When You Believe." *Vogue* called their finale a "joyous tribute to unity, hope, and peace."

LEFT A poster for *Wicked* features Ariana as Glinda. The film was released on November 22, 2024, to wide acclaim and rave reviews, for the film itself and for Ariana and her co-stars' performances.

It's an incredible privilege to be a part of this version of it and to have it be so accessible to so many people. . . . I think so many new theater kids have been born."

—ARIANA ON *FRESH AIR*, FEBRUARY 4, 2025

LEFT Ariana and Cynthia Erivo gaze into a mirror as Ariana's character, Galinda, attempts to give Erivo's character, Elphaba, a tone-deaf makeover. "We provided each other with the space and the kindness and generosity that was necessary to play these kinds of roles," Erivo said in an interview at the Red Sea Film Fest in December 2024. "To sing with another person is a very intimate thing," she added.

RIGHT Director Jon M. Chu breaks down a scene with Ariana and Cynthia on the set of *Wicked*. Chu has talked about his original hesitation in casting Ariana for the role before watching her "transform" during her auditions. "I felt like I was meeting Galinda for the first time, not Ariana Grande."

LEFT Cynthia Erivo and Ariana attend the Los Angeles premiere of *Wicked* at Dorothy Chandler Pavilion on November 9, 2024. Erivo and Ariana hit the promotional ground running, with appearances across the globe. The two often wore outfits reflecting the colors associated with their characters.

RIGHT Ariana and partner, Ethan Slater, share a moment at the 31st Annual Screen Actors Guild Awards at the Shrine Auditorium in Los Angeles on February 23, 2025. The two met on the set of *Wicked*, in which Slater played Boq Woodsman. Rumors swirled around the two when they were first publicly named a couple.

LEFT Michelle Yeoh, Jon M. Chu, Ariana, Jeff Goldblum, Marc E. Platt, and Cynthia Erivo celebrate the movie's win backstage during the 82nd Golden Globes held in Beverly Hills in January 2025. The film was nominated for four Golden Globes, winning one for Cinematic and Box Office Achievement.

RIGHT Ariana looks serene on the red carpet at the Golden Globes. In a post about her nomination for best performance by a female actor in a supporting role, she said she was "floored," continuing, "I am simply so deeply grateful for this acknowledgment."

ABOVE Ariana prepares to go onstage at the 97th Academy Awards at the Dolby Theater held on March 2, 2025, in Hollywood. In a nod to Judy Garland, the original Dorothy and Ariana's lifelong inspiration, she wears a ruby sequined Schiaparelli dress with a ruby slipper at the back.

RIGHT Ariana achieves new heights at the 97th Oscars, singing "Over the Rainbow" to open the night's festivities.

[I told her], 'You deserve this, and it's time for the world to see you in this.' I honestly can't wait for the world to see her nail this part."

–KRISTIN CHENOWETH–GLINDA IN
THE ORIGINAL STAGE VERSION OF *WICKED*–
TO ABC, SEPTEMBER 4, 2023

ABOVE In addition to the female gender sign on her middle finger (photographed here as she arrives at the 31st Annual Screen Actors Guild Awards in LA in February 2025), Ariana has over seventy tattoos, almost all with personal meanings. The gender sign was inked on the same night as an "A" on her left thumb. She got both tattoos with her late boyfriend, Mac Miller. As a tribute to the city of Manchester, which is symbolized by the worker bee, she also has a bee tattoo behind her left ear.

RIGHT In a rare *Wicked* appearance with no trace of pink, Ariana wears a little black dress from Emporio Armani at CinemaCon 2025, where the first trailer for *Wicked: For Good* debuted in April.

> **"Every time she came in, she was the most interesting person. You just couldn't take your eyes away."**
>
> –JON M. CHU ON ARIANA'S AUDITIONS FOR GLINDA TO *VANITY FAIR*, SEPTEMBER 30, 2024

A Closer Look
RED-CARPET STYLE

After several years out of the public spotlight, Ariana eagerly took on the promotion of *Wicked*, with all the requisite red-carpet events. She went more high fashion than her typical outfits, collaborating with couture houses like Loewe and Louis Vuitton, and adding many subtle and overt nods to her character, Glinda the Good Witch. Pale pinks and greens predominated, with an occasional Dorothy-esque gingham thrown into the mix. High-fashion fans await the second installment of *Wicked* and the red-carpet looks that will surely accompany it.

> " [Ariana's] always struck that balance of having that girl next door *je ne sais quoi* and also having an iconic, recognizable image."
>
> —AAMINA INAYAT KHAN, STYLECASTER, NOVEMBER 21, 2024

Ariana makes her first public appearance for *Wicked* in a short Oscar de la Renta dress made up of fabric petals during CinemaCon at Caesars Palace on April 10, 2024, in Las Vegas.

RIGHT Ariana attends the Australian premiere of *Wicked* on November 3, 2024, in Sydney. Vivienne Westwood designed her diaphanous pink gown, a nod to the original Glinda from 1939's *The Wizard of Oz*.

For the Los Angeles premiere of *Wicked*, on November 9, 2024, Ariana opts for a pink gingham, Oz-inspired custom dress designed by Thom Browne.

149

Ariana attends a special screening of *Wicked* at the Museum of Modern Art on November 14, 2024, in New York, in a hot-pink off-the-shoulder Louis Vuitton dress.

Wrapped in a light-lemon-yellow custom silk dress from the Ralph Lauren Collection, Ariana appears at the European premiere at the Royal Festival Hall on November 18, 2024, in London.

Ariana goes way outside her box of pastels in a loose-fitting black dress from the Row at the SAG-AFTRA Foundation screening of *Wicked* on December 4, 2024, in New York.

Ariana is in vintage Chanel Haute Couture at *Variety*'s Creative Impact Awards on January 4, 2025, in Palm Springs.

Ariana channels the spirit of Glinda in a pale-green satin Louis Vuitton strapless gown with bubble skirt at the Palm Springs International Film Festival in January 2025.

For the 82nd Golden Globes at the Beverly Hilton on January 5, 2025, Ariana opts for an archival pale-yellow empire-waist column gown with a beaded bodice from the 1966 collection by Hubert de Givenchy.

For the National Board of Review Gala on January 7, 2025, in New York, Ariana sports Loewe. The baby-pink satin gown featured darting at the front and a matching shawl for an old-Hollywood vibe.

At the 30th Critics' Choice Awards at Barker Hangar on February 7, 2025, in Santa Monica, California, Ariana stuns in a Dior cage dress. The dress had a fringe hem and was covered in floral appliques.

At the 40th Annual Santa Barbara International Film Festival: Virtuosos on February 9, 2025, Ariana returns to pastels in a Glinda-pink frothy ball gown from Armani Privè's fall/winter 2022 couture collection.

Ariana continues to channel Glinda at the EE BAFTA Film Awards on February 16, 2025, in London in a custom Louis Vuitton gown with plunging neckline and poofy bubblegum-pink skirt.

Ariana attends the 31st Annual Screen Actors Guild Awards at the Shrine Auditorium and Expo Hall on February 23, 2025, in Los Angeles. She dons a custom light-pink gown from Loewe with cascading feather flowers.

For the 97th Annual Academy Awards Nominees Dinner at the Academy Museum of Motion Pictures on February 25, 2025, in Los Angeles, Ariana arrives in archival Yves Saint Laurent from the house's fall 1991 haute couture collection.

THE FAMILY GIRL

FROM THE START, Ariana's mom, Joan Grande, has been a guiding light and supporter. A businesswoman, she modeled both grit and loyalty—moving their family to Boca Raton from New York when she was eight months pregnant with Ariana, and then moving across the country to support Ariana's dreams. She instilled in her daughter a love for all things horror and goth, as well as a passion for musicals and R&B.

Joan was with Ariana at the Manchester concert and stayed by her side when they returned to Boca and then traveled back to Manchester for the tribute concert. And she remains by Ariana's side today. In an interview with *ET* outside the 82nd Golden Globe Awards, Ariana said of her mom, "We're together, always."

"She's magnificent in every way," said Joan. "It's inside, outside, in everything she does." To which Ariana tearfully replied, "Thank you, Mom."

Ariana and her mom, Joan, pose at their home in Los Angeles on March 31, 2012.

TOP LEFT Ariana and her grandmother, Marjorie, attend the MTV Video Music Awards at the Forum on August 24, 2014, in Inglewood, California. By the time *Wicked* premiered, Marjorie was ninety-eight and traveling less, so Ariana brought *Wicked* to her. They took in the film at the local theater Ariana and her brother, Frankie, had gone to as children. In 2025 Marjorie became the oldest person to chart in *Billboard*'s Top 100 as a result of Ariana sampling her voice in the song "Ordinary Things."

ABOVE During the MTV Video Music Awards at Radio City Music Hall on August 20, 2018, in New York City. Ariana invites important women in her life—her grandmother, her mother, and (not pictured) her cousin Lani—onstage with her.

LEFT Ariana attends the American Music Awards on November 22, 2015, in Los Angeles, accompanied by her brother, her grandmother, and her mother.

LEFT Ariana dances onstage at the first night of her two-night run at Madison Square Garden during the Dangerous Woman Tour. Both shows, on February 23 and 24, 2017, featured support from Little Mix and Victoria Monét.

FAR RIGHT Ariana performs at the iHeartRadio Jingle Ball in 2013. She'd just released *Yours Truly* a few months before and was already a platinum-record recipient and best-selling artist.

**HEARST
HOME**

Copyright © 2025 by
Hearst Magazine Media, Inc.
All rights reserved.

Jacqueline Deval, VP, PUBLISHER
Nicole Fisher, DEPUTY DIRECTOR
Maria Ramroop, DEPUTY
MANAGING EDITOR
Laurene Chavez, ART DIRECTOR
Cinzia Reale-Castello, SENIOR
PHOTO EDITOR

PRODUCED BY ONE+ONE BOOKS

Gillian MacLeod, DESIGNER
Shayna Ian, PHOTO RESEARCHER
Laura Whittemore, COPYEDITOR
Carrie Wicks, PROOFREADER

Library of Congress
Cataloging-in-Publication Data
Available on request

10 9 8 7 6 5 4 3 2 1

Published by Hearst Home,
an imprint of Hearst Books/
Hearst Magazine Media, Inc.
300 W 57th Street
New York, NY 10019

Hearst Home, the Hearst
Home logo, and Hearst Books
are registered trademarks of
Hearst Communications, Inc.

For information about custom
editions, special sales, premium,
and corporate purchases:
hearst.com/magazines/
hearst-books

Printed in Canada

978-1-958395-56-1

PHOTO CREDITS Cover AB + DM/AUGUST. Back Cover Matt Crossick/ Empics/Alamy Live News. John Shearer/Getty Images for The Recording Academy 2, 104 Samir Hussein/Wireimage 5 Karwai Tang/WireImage 6, 150 (right) Vikpit/Shutterstock 7 (bottom) Andrew Francis Wallace/Toronto Star via Getty Images 9 Kevin Mazur/Getty Images for Republic Records 10, 158 Kevin Mazur/MG24/Getty Images for The Met Museum/Vogue 13, 109, 113 (bottom), 136-137 GeorgePeters/Getty Images 14 (top left) Bruce Glikas/ FilmMagic 14 (top right), 36, 39, 41, 42, 72-73 Kevin Mazur/Getty Images for AG 14 (bottom), 20, 67, 98-99, 100-101, 102 (left), 102 (right), 103 (top), 103 (bottom), 125, 160 Jim Spellman/Contributor/Getty Images 15 Nickelodeon Productions/Album/Alamy Stock Photo 16 (left) NurPhoto/NurPhoto via Getty Images 17 David M. Benett/Dave Benett/Getty Images for Ariana Grande Fragrance 18 Dave Hogan for One Love Manchester/Getty Images 19 (top), 119 Giles Keyte/©Universal Pictures/Courtesy Everett Collection 21, 132-133, 139 (bottom) Kevin Winter/Getty Images 22-23 Walter McBride/ Corbis via Getty Images 24, 35, 70 (bottom) INDECcraft/Getty Images 25 (bottom), 61 (bottom) Jesse Grant/WireImage 26 Micah Smith/Getty Images 29, 38 (bottom), 40, 156 Pictorial Press Ltd/Alamy Stock Photo 30 FOX Image Collection via Getty Images 32 Terence Patrick/CBS via Getty Images 33 (top) Beth Corey Dubber/©Showtime/Courtesy Everett Collection 33 (bottom) Dario Cantatore/Getty Images 37 Paul Archuleta/FilmMagic 38 (top), 79 Frazer Harrison/Getty Images 43, 155 (right) Araya Diaz/Getty Images for Nickelodeon 44-45 Kevin Mazur/KCA2014/WireImage 46 Frazer Harrison/ KCA2014/Getty Images 47 Universal Pictures Television/Warner Bros./Album/ Alamy Stock Photo 48-49 Hyperobject Industries/Album/Alamy Stock Photo 50-51 Rich Polk/Penske Media via Getty Images 53 (top), 114, 145 Tommaso Boddi/FilmMagic 53 (bottom left) Don Arnold/WireImage 53 (bottom right) Jason LaVeris/FilmMagic 54 James Devaney/WireImage 55 (left) Jason Merritt/Getty Images for MTV 55 (right) Steve Granitz/WireImage 56 (left), 58 (left) Angela Weiss/AFP via Getty Images 57 (right) 68 (bottom right), 134 Gotham/Getty Images 59 (left) Gregg DeGuire/Penske Media via Getty Images 59 (right) Kevin Mazur/Getty Images for Live Nation 60, 64, Kevin Mazur/Getty Images for The Recording Academy 63 Kevin Mazur/WireImage 68 (top left), 90-91, 113 (top), 157 (top left), 157 (top right) C Flanigan/Getty Images 68 (top right) Allen Berezovsky/WireImage 68 (bottom left) Kevin Winter/MTV VMAs 2020/Getty Images for MTV 69 (middle right), 106 Gilbert Carrasquillo/GC Images 69 (left) John Nacion/Variety via Getty Images 69 (bottom right) Jason Merritt/WireImage 71 Jeff Kravitz/FilmMagic for MTV 74 SAV/FilmMagic 75 Ian Gavan/Getty Images for MTV 77 Kevin Winter/ MTV1415/Getty Images for MTV 78 Jeff Kravitz/AMA2014/FilmMagic 81, 110 Jason Merritt/Getty Images for iHeartMedia 82 Michael Tran/FilmMagic 83 Kevork Djansezian/Getty Images 84-85 Brill/ullstein bild via Getty Images 86-87 Kevin Mazur/AMA2016/WireImage 88 Jeff Kravitz/FilmMagic 89, 93 (bottom), 155 (left) Kevin Winter/Getty Images for iHeartMedia 92, 129 (bottom) Noam Galai/WireImage 93 (top) Kevin Mazur/Getty Images for American Express 94 Kevin Mazur/Getty Images for Ariana Grande 95, 116 Kevin Mazur/Getty Images for *Billboard* 96-97 Monty Brinton/CBS via Getty Images 105 Jeff Kravitz/AMA2016/FilmMagic 111 Kevin Mazur/One Love Manchester/Getty Images for One Love Manchester 112, 126-127 kampee patisena/Getty Images 115 (bottom) Theo Wargo/Getty Images 120 Retro AdArchives/Alamy Stock Photo 122 Cindy Ord/Getty Images for iHeartRadio 123 (top right), Barry King/Alamy Stock Photo 123 (top left) Kevin Mazur/ Getty Images for Coburn Communications 123 (bottom) Christopher Polk/ Getty Images 124 (top) GC Images 124 (bottom) Mark Sagliocco/FilmMagic 128 David Livingston/Getty Images 129 (top) Giles Keyte/NBC/Universal 131 Marleen Moise/Getty Images 135 BFA/Universal Pictures/Alamy Stock Photo 138 Giles Keyte/NBC/Universal 139 (top) Axelle/ Bauer-Griffin/FilmMagic 140, 149 (right), 153 (right) Presley Ann Photo/Shutterstock for SAG 141 Ellen von Unwerth/GG2025/ Penske Media via Getty Images 142 JC Olivera/GG2025/Penske Media via Getty Images 143, 152 (right) John Shearer/97th Oscars/The Academy via Getty Images 144 Robyn Beck/AFP via Getty Images 146 Gilbert Flores/Variety via Getty Images 147 Jerod Harris/Getty Images for CinemaCon 148 Don Arnold/WireImage 149 (left) Roy Rochlin/Getty Images for Universal Pictures 150 (left) Dominik Bindl/Getty Images 151 (left) David Crotty/Patrick McMullan via Getty Images 151 (right) Matt Winkelmeyer/Getty Images for Palm Springs International Film Society 152 (left) TheStewartofNY/ FilmMagic 153 (left) Robin L Marshall/WireImage 154 (left) Mike Marsland/ WireImage 154 (right) Frazer Harrison/AMA2015/Getty Images for dcp 157 (bottom) David Moffly/Alamy Stock Photo 159

Ariana sparkles
onstage at Coachella
on April 14, 2019.
She finished her
night headlining
with an encore of
"Thank U, Next."